PLACE NAMES IN THE WRITINGS OF
WILLIAM BUTLER YEATS

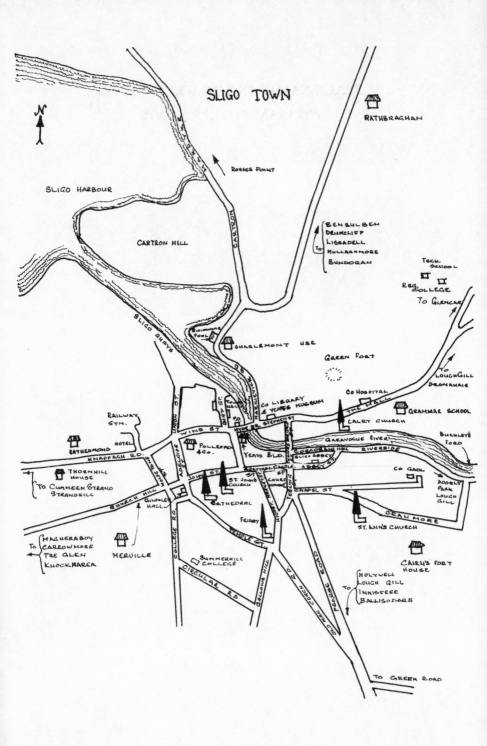

PLACE NAMES
IN THE WRITINGS OF
WILLIAM BUTLER YEATS

by
James P. McGarry

edited and with additional material by
Edward Malins

and a Preface by
Kathleen Raine

MACMILLAN OF CANADA
MACLEAN-HUNTER PRESS

First published in Great Britain by Colin Smythe Ltd.

First published in North America by The Macmillan Company
of Canada Limited. 1976

ISBN 0–7705–1468–5

Printed in England
for the Macmillan Company of Canada Limited
Toronto, Ontario M5B 1X3

PREFACE

When first I began to know Ireland (through the annual Yeats summer-school) two people acted for me the part of Sligo's hosts. The first was Sheelah Kirby (author of *The Yeats Country*) who had a knowledge of her native county, its historic and pre-historic sites gained not from books but from living with them. She was the guide to many besides myself who came to those Sligo summer-schools, in part to pay tribute to Yeats but also because in Ireland we found everywhere those living memories that consecrate places, a sense of national identity associated with river and mountain, that in our own countries had long been obliterated by the indifferent bull-dozers of 'progress'.

My other host was James McGarry, whose Sunday outings were always carefully planned to include something out of the ordinary; not places only, but also people. He it was who introduced me not only to the Castle of Heroes on Lough Key, but also to the old boatman to whom the entwined trunks of two trees on the graves of 'Una bhan' and 'Proud Costello', on Trinity Island, were a living testimony of the undying love of a pair celebrated in Irish song. The old boatman in whose memory so many old poems, so much living tradition was enshrined did not long survive the felling of the trees by a party intent on clearing the site of the ancient church. On another Sunday, "on Cruachan's windy plain" an English friend and I nervously watched a live bull advancing on us as our host (he had his back to the herd) told us, on that ancient site of Queen Maeve's Court, of the white-horned bull and the brown bull of the *Tain*. With him I visited the long-neglected (but now honoured) grave of the last of the bards, O'Carolan, whose harp is kept now in Clonalis, in Koscommon, the house of O'Conor Don (The Rev. Clark O'Connor, S.J.) and

5

his sister, Miss Josephine O'Connor; last of the line of those hereditary High Kings for whom the great poet and harper sang, composed and played.

Another year we visited Lady Gregory's deserted garden, its old Irish Yews and catalpa trees dripping with rain. On the way we stopped to call upon the son of the farmer who had taught Irish to Lady Gregory and to Douglas Hyde. Handling the worn grammar-book I seemed to understand why Yeats has "delighted in every age where poet and artist confined themselves gladly to some inherited subject-matter known to a whole people."

It is with intent that Yeats names in his poetry places and people who belong to Ireland's living inheritance; names deeply rooted in the national being of a people before the poet shared Thoor Ballylee with the jackdaws or was laid to rest under the old stone cross at Drumcliff. He built on the strong foundations of inherited tradition, adding to places already made holy by some legend of saint or hero new significance. Other names he himself added: Innisfree and Lissadell, dear to his own childhood and youth. Others again, like Lady Gregory's Coole Park with its seven woods and lake of the wild swans, or Rosses Point (the "Memory Harbour" of his brother the painter Jack Yeats) were made memorable by what Yeats and his friends there accomplished.

No stranger to Ireland, no professional historian or archaeologist could have written this book. James McGarry has gathered exact knowledge, over many years, less from books than from local knowledge. Only this summer I was with him at Usna, whose "cat stone" is called "the navel of Ireland", for there the four Provinces meet and there the ancient High Kings received tribute. We stopped by the road to ask directions from an old man waiting for the bus. He told us the way, adding that he himself remembered the day de Valera had held a rally on the place called "the bed of St Patrick". Kings, saint, and the heroic history of recent years flowed in a single stream.

Mr Edward Malins, who has made valuable contributions to Yeats studies, and is also an authority on Irish country houses, has edited and supplemented Mr McGarry's text from his own specialised knowledge. But I write this preface in personal gratitude to James McGarry who has over the years shown me so

6

much more than the outward shell of houses, ruin or ancient grave; and in the hope and belief that this book will serve as guide to whoever wishes to make their pilgrimage of those historic, heroic, Christian and pre-Christian holy places whose names Yeats chose, with deliberation, to fashion into his work. In so doing he was performing the role of the ancient Irish *fili* (bardic poets) whose task it was to perpetuate in the memory, men and heroic acts; as Homer has made the names of Ithaca, Chios and Troy places of imagination for generations who never visited Greece.

Kathleen Raine, D.Litt.

Note: the page references
given throughout this book
are for the English editions
of W. B. Yeats's writings.

AUTHORS' NOTE

In deciding which places should be included in this volume we have confined ourselves to entries for those places actually mentioned by W. B. Yeats in the standard editions of his works – *Collected Poems, Collected Plays. Autobiographies, Explorations, Mythologies, Essays and Introductions, A Vision* – together with *On the Boiler* and those poems of Yeats's not in *Collected Poems*, but which appear on pp. 641–792 of *The Variorum Edition of the Poems of W. B. Yeats*, and the notes and Prefaces and Dedications in that volume (pp. 793–857).

With one or two exceptions we have not included places which Yeats described but did not name. There are so many which are impossible to identify from the information available, that we could not hope to provide anything like a complete listing.

This book was first started as an aid for the reader of Yeats's writings, so that he or she could have a ready reference volume other than Saul's *Prolegomena** to the Poems and to the Plays, which may not provide complete or accurate information. But we then decided to add the page references at the end of each entry, as we thought these would be of interest and value to the general reader as well as the student of Yeats's writings. However, we left out the page references to Sligo and Dublin as they appear so often, thirty-five for the former and seventy for the latter.

We have used the following abbreviations for the books:

A   *Autobiographies* (Macmillan 1955)
M   *Mythologies* (Macmillan 1959)
CP   *Collected Poems* (Macmillan (1950)
VP   *Variorum Edition of the Poems* (Macmillan 1957)
Pl   *Collected Plays* (Macmillan 1952)

*See pp. 94—7 for a list of corrections.

9

Ex   *Explorations* (Macmillan 1962)
E&I   *Essays & Introductions* (Macmillan 1961)
B   *On the Boiler* (Cuala Press 1939)
V   *A Vision* (Macmillan 1937, and with corrections 1962)
We have also used the letters FM to refer to the 17th century work known as *The Annals of the Four Masters*.

There are variant spellings of many of the place names that Yeats referred to, both in his writings and elsewhere. We have given his spellings in capital letters in each entry, and then given alternative and/or correct versions. It is probable that Yeats and Lady Gregory took down local place names from informants who would not have been certain of the spelling themselves, and there were often local variants in spelling and pronunciation. For example 'Kyle-na-dyfe' as used by Lady Gregory is the same place as 'Kinadife' mentioned by Yeats, and Aughanish, is pronounced Aughnish in some areas. For this reason we have not attempted to give the reader any idea of the correct pronunciation of the Irish versions.

Where possible, English translations of the Irish names are given, together with details of Irish history or myth relating to the place, which we consider is helpful for a full appreciation of Yeats's writing and hope may lead to an understanding of his use of the name.

We are most grateful to all whose local knowledge has been of such great help in the preparation of this book, and to Bord Failte, and the Commissioners of Public Work in Ireland for their assistance in providing the illustrations.

JIM McGARRY
EDWARD MALINS

April 1976

CONTENTS

Preface by Kathleen Raine   5

Authors' Note   9

Place Names in the Writings of W. B. Yeats   15

Bibliography   92

Appendices

1. Notes on G. B. Saul's *Prolegomena*   94

2. Ancient Names for Ireland   98

3. A Note on Pronunciation   99

ILLUSTRATIONS

The Abbey Theatre, Dublin (a)
Thoor Ballylee (a)
Coole Park (c)
Lissadell (a)
The Autograph Tree at Coole (a)
Glencar Waterfall (a)
Castle Island, Lough Kay (a)
Lough Gill (a)
Poulnabrone Dolmen (a)
Gallerus Oratory (a)
Rock of Cashel (b)
Corcomroe Abbey (b)
Crianan Ailich Fort (b)
Dun Aengus, Innishmore (a)
The Catstone on Usnach Hill (b)
Megalithic Tomb at Moytirra East (b)
Knocknarea and Lough Gill (a)
O'Rourke's Castle (d)
The Hawk's Rock at Tullaghan (a)
Drumcliff Cross (a)
W. B. Yeats's grave and Ben Bulben (a)

Acknowledgements for the use of these photos are as follows :

(a) Bord Failte
(b) Commissioners of Public Works in Ireland
(c) Colin Smythe
(d) James P. McGarry

ABBEY Townland in the Burren, County Clare, divided into Abbey East and Abbey West; adjoins townlands of Oughmama and Bel Harbour, (Bealaclugga). One of several townlands referred to in *The Dreaming of the Bones*, all in neighbourhood of Corcomroe Abbey where the play is set. Pl. 434.

ABBEY OF WHITE FRIARS Abbey Street, Sligo. Not an abbey but a friary. Built 1253 by Maurice FitzGerald for Dominicans. Well preserved ruin with many interesting features, best known the 17th O'Conor memorial. Sacked by Sir Frederick Hamilton in 1641. M. 147, 148, 177.

ABBEY THEATRE corner of Lower Abbey Street and Marlborough Street, Dublin. Opened as the Irish National Theatre on 27 December 1904, so giving a permanent home to the Irish Literary Theatre founded by Yeats, Lady Gregory and Edward Martyn : first performance was of *On Baile's Strand* and Lady Gregory's comedy, *Spreading the News*. From that date, plays were chosen irrespective of whether they pleased or enraged Irish Nationalists, English censors or the Castle. Eventually a team of actors and stage staff brought to the Abbey a living theatre and poetic drama such as could not be equalled anywhere else in Europe. But for them the plays of Synge, O'Casey, Lady Gregory, Yeats, Hyde and many others might never have been seen. It was a great practical achievement on Yeats' and Lady Gregory's part for they bore the brunt of the administration. Accidentally destroyed by fire in 1951. Reopened 1966 in a new building by Michael Scott. A. 398, 491, 505, 514, 537, 557, 567. B. 13, 14, 28, 32, 33, 34. CP. 107, 348. M. 345. Ex. 124, 164, 181, 187, 190, 199, 222, 226, 227, 240, 244, 246, 247, 248,, 269, 339, 414, 444, 445, 447. E&I. 305, 319, 523.

ACADEMY OF MUSIC now the Royal Irish Academy of Music, 36 Westland Row, Dublin. Built 1771. Restored 1956. Academy founded 1856. M. 75.

ALLEN. Hill of. See ALMHUIN.

ALMHUIN Allmhuin or Sid Almhain. The Hill of Allen, 8 miles

N.E. of Kildare, County Kildare. Prominent hill rising 676 feet from flat country, the other-world dwelling of the god Nuada. Palace of Finn Mac Cumhaill (Cool), referred to in many old Gaelic stories. Finn brought Grainne here after the death of Diarmuid on Ben Bulben. Many mounds and raths. One of three residences of the King of Leinster. Saga of Battle of Allen. C.P. 414, 430. Pl. 110. Ex. 14, 15, 28, 29.

ALT The Glen on the side of Knocknarea, County Sligo. See GLEN CP. 393.

ANTIENT CONCERT ROOMS now the Academy Cinema in Pearse Street, formerly Brunswick Street, Dublin. First performances of *The Countess Cathleen*, and *The Heather Field* by Edward Martyn here in May 1899, inaugurating the Irish Literary Theatre. Strong Catholic demonstrations all week against Yeats' play. James Joyce sang *Down by the Salley Gardens* at a concert on 27th August 1904 with John McCormack also participating. Yeats and Padraic Pearse lectured there (1914), on Thomas Davis one of the leaders of the Young Ireland Movement and co-founder of *The Nation*, having been banned from Trinity College by the Vice-Provost, Dr Mahaffy. A. 414, 452, 454. Ex. 86, 88.

ARAN Ara – Three Aran Islands off the coast of Galway – Inishmoore, Inishmaan and Inisheer. Important antiquarian centres, in particular their caiseals or stone forts of which Dun Aenghus is the most famous, dramatically situated on a cliff edge by prehistoric man, allegedly the Fir Bolg. (Belgic Celts). Mother and step-mother of the Children of Lir were the daughters of Ailil of Ara. In Ireland's Golden Age renowned for monastic settlements. Associated with John Millington Synge, Robert O'Flaherty and Liam O'Flaherty (a native.) Gaelic is the speech on account of the relative isolation of the islands. A. 321, 343, 569. B. 15. V. 167, 222. Pl. 434, 435, 443, 565, 569. Ex. 31, 32, 50, 68, 192, 249, 418. E&I. 51, 167, 232, 299, 324, 334.

ARDRAHAN Ard-Rathain, ferny heights, County Galway, a hamlet on Galway–Limerick road 8 m. N. of Gort. Striking ruin of 13th c. castle built on a fort. Nearby, Isertkelly and Laban. M. 26. A. 425. Pl. 434.

ARTS CLUB, United Arts Club, formerly in Upper Merrion Street, now at 3 Upper Fitzwilliam Street, Dublin. A. 461, 476, 480.

ARTS SCHOOLS IN KILDARE STREET, DUBLIN ART SCHOOLS, Metropolitan School of Art, between Stephens Green and Nassau Street, Dublin. In part of National Library Buildings. When Yeats left the Erasmus Smith High School he enrolled (May 1884–July 1885) as a student in the Arts School, in which his father was a teacher. It was here Yeats first met George Russell – A.E. A. 79, 158, 468. Ex. 193. E&I. 4, 412.

ATHENRY Ath-na-Riogh, the ford of the kings. Once a strategic centre in County Galway. In 1316 one of the decisive battles of Irish history was fought outside the town when young Felim O'Conor, King of Connacht (the Flower of Connacht) perished in the Edward Bruce campaign against the Anglo-Normans, the victors. Thereafter walled town; much of the walls and one of its gates still standing. Interesting ruins, 13th c. de Bermingham castle and Dominican friary. M. 46.

AUBEG Awbeg, County Cork. Abhann Beag, little river. Yeats is correct in thinking it is the Mulla of Edmund Spenser, but inaccurate in quoting 'The Faerie Queene': Bk IV Canto XI.41. which should be 'And Mulla mine, whose waves I whilom taught to weep'. He also knows the Mulla as 'daughter of Old Mole' from Spenser's 'Colin Clout's Come Home Againe' 1. 108. The Awbeg flows through the Annagh Bog, bends its course to Buttevant, afterwards to Doneraile through the territories which were owned by Spenser, before it joins the Avonmore or Blackwater. E&I. 360.

AUGHANISH (pronounced Aughnish) Ough-innis, Each-Inis – the promontory of the horse; Six miles N.W. of Kinvarra, N. County Clare : 'inis' usually means 'island' but is sometimes used as here, for a peninsula or promontory. Pl. 370, 437.

17

AUGHRIM Each-dhruim, the hill or ridge of the horse, a small village near Ballinasloe, County Galway; the scene of the Battle of Aughrim, (1691) which effectively ended the Jacobite–Williamite War in Ireland. Pl. 683.

AUGHTMANA Oughtmama, County Galway, the breast of the mountain pass. Valley near Corcomroe Abbey where St Colman retired, after resigning his See of Kilmacduagh, and founded a monastery. Many cahirs, cairns and caves. Ruins of three churches. The end of Bothar na Mias, The Way of the Dishes. Pl. 437.

AVENA HOUSE Ballysadare, County Sligo, where William Middleton, grand uncle of Yeats lived, and where Yeats listened in the kitchen to the stories of Paddy Flynn, the gardener. At the rear, Yeats frequently sat on a large rock in the river looking across at the Salley Gardens (see SALLEY GARDENS) and the Mill Field where he rode the piebald pony. A. 76.

BAILE'S STRAND County Louth, Fraigh mbaile in the story of Baile Mac Buain; suburb of Dundalk, now known as Seatown, near the fort alleged to be the home of Cuchulain. Pl. 245, 699, 701. A. 436, 449. E&I. 233.

BAILEVELEHAN Ballyvelaghan, Baile-Ui-Mhaolachain, the place of the pathway, N. County Clare, between New Quay and Corcomroe. Pl. 437.

BALLINA Bel-atha-an-fheadha, the ford of the mouth of the wood, on the Moy estuary, County Mayo, a market town and small seaport. On the outskirts of Ballina is Ardnaree, Ard-na-raghadh, the hill of the executions from a 7th c. story of the hangings there of the four Maols, foster brothers of St Grellan and Guaire the Hospitable, King of Connacht. Friary founded by the O'Dowds in the 14th c. Franciscan friary nearby. A. 10, 67, 70. Pl. 77, 78, 81.

BALLINAFAD Bel-an-atha-fada, the mouth of the long ford, County Sligo, at foot of Curlew mountains and beside

Lough Arrow. A secondary road still known as The Red Earl's Road or Bothar an Iarla Ruadh, from 13th c. Red Earl of Ulster (de Burgo). Remains of 17th c. Plantation Castle built to guard the entrance to County Sligo. Nearby, the ruins of Aghanagh Church, erected on site of one founded by St Patrick; Bricklieve Mountain, one of the most famous megalithic sites in Ireland; Hollybrook, the setting of *Willy Reilly and his fair Colleen Bawn*, immortalised by William Carleton. C.P. 25.

BALLAGHADEREEN Ballaghaderreen, Bealach an Doirin, the road of the little oak wood, County Roscommon. The cathedral town of the Diocese of Achonry. The home of John Dillon, a leader of the Irish Party and one of the founders of the Land League (1879). Before boundary changes, in Co. Mayo. Ex. 98.

BALLISODARE (or Ballysadare) County Sligo, formerly Eas Dara, later Baile-Eas-Dara. Usually translated as the town of the cataract of the oak, but O'Donovan ascribed the name to a Formonian druid named Dara who was slain there by Lewy of the Long Hand. The Formonians are alleged to have landed in Ballysadare Bay. In 6th c. a meeting there of the Saints of Ireland with Columcille. Remains of 7th c. church founded by St Fechin, and 13th c. Dominican church on the site of the silver mines (now disused).

The Pollexfens' mills situated there on both sides of the Owenmore river which drove the mill wheels. William Middleton, grand-uncle of Yeats, lived in Avena House. Ballisodare is a famous privately owned salmon fishery where salmon poaching has been elevated to an art, celebrated in the ballad, 'The Boys of Ballysadare'. A. 15, 16, 76, 78. M. 5.

BALLYGAWLEY more correctly Ballydawley, Baile Dhalaigh, the townland of O'Daly about five miles from Sligo. Ballygawley Lake has an island formerly a crannog. M. 241, 243, 245. Pl. 68.

BALLYLEE Baile-an-Liagh, Baile ui Laoi, County Galway. The townland in which Thoor Ballylee is situated, three miles from Gort on the link road to Coole; 'Tor' meaning tower. Acquired its name from a family named Leech, O'Liagh, hereditary 'leeches' to the O'Flaherties of Iar Connacht (Connemara). *The Book of the O'Liaigh* (1443) is a large vellum MS written in Irish and Latin, and now in the Royal Irish Academy library.

Thoor Ballylee is a sturdy medieval tower guarding a stone bridge which was once a fording place over a swift-flowing stream. The interior is simple : four storeys, each one large room, a narrow stair cut into the walls, and battlements as parapet. The setting had associations with Mary Hynes and the blind poet Raftery who had loved her. In 1917, even though the doors were rotten and there was no roof on the tower, Yeats made a bid for the property, then owned by the government. As no one wanted it he managed to buy it and the two cottages for £35. Then he set to work to have repairs done, and sturdy elm furniture was designed and made on the spot by craftsmen from Gort. In the summer of 1919 he and his wife were able to take up residence there, but the tower's ground floor room was flooded when the river was high, so they were able to live there only during the summer months. For some years previously the symbol of the tower as the place in which he might search for wisdom had been used by him; and it is integral to the poems of 'The Tower' period.

After the summer of 1929 the Yeatses did not again live in Thoor Ballylee, and although they owned it nothing was done to keep it in repair. Vandals tore planks from the oak door and water poured through the roof. Thanks to the splendid work of Mrs Mary Hanley of Limerick and the Kiltartan Society, aided by Bord Failte Eireann, restoration has taken place and the buildings are now in excellent condition. M. 22, 23, 24, 25, 26. CP. 180, 218, 229, 230, 275. A. 561.

BALLYLEE Baile-an-Liaigh, County Galway. Two townlands named Ballylee mentioned by Yeats but there are in fact three townlands of the name in that county. The one referred to in "The Death of Hanrahan" (see ref. below) is at the foot of Slieve Echtghe on the road from Loughrea to Gort. An ideal place for Yeats and Lady Gregory to search for the Hidden Ireland. All the places in and about Echtghe were on the Persse estate (Lady Gregory's family estate at Roxborough). M. 253.

BALLYMONEY Baile-Mhuine, the town of the shrubbery on the river Bann, County Antrim. Pl. 597.

BELFAST Beal Feirste, mouth of the sandpit (crossing the river Lagan) capital of Northern Ireland and Ireland's largest seaport and manufacturing area; at head of Belfast Lough, Loch Loig. Of 17th c. origin, built beside an old ford. Charter of James I in 1613; Huguenot settlement later in 17th c. Made a City in 1888 by Queen Victoria. Ironically, Belfast was the cradle of the Society of United Irishmen and of Irish Republicanism. Only mentioned *en passant* by Yeats. E&I. 311. A. 222. Pl. 602.

BELFAST UNIVERSITY. Queen's University, Belfast. Founded 1845, as Queen's College; granted University Charter in 1908. Pl. 603.

BELSHRAGH County Galway. Belsragh Lake locally known as Resragh; small lake on the top of Slieve Echgthe at the Loughrea end. Belsragh and Restragh mean the mouth and the end of the swampy meadow respectively. M. 253.

BELTRA STRAND – Beal Traigh – the mouth of the strand, County Sligo. Called Triagh Eotail in *The Battle of Moytirra*. See Moytirra.

BEN BULBEN, Beann Ghulban, Binn Gulbain, Gulban's Peak in North County Sligo, where Conall Gulban, a son of Nial of the Nine Hostages, was fostered. He was the ancestor of the O'Donnells of Donegal from which the district got the name Tirconnell. Eachtra Chonaill Ghulban (16th c.) describes the adventures in eastern lands of Conal Gulban. It is the scene of the wild boar hunt at which Diarmuid was killed in The Elopement of Diarmuid and Grainne, and The Battle of the Books (Cuil Dreimbhe) Cooladrummon, 561 A.D. fought as a result of the first case of copyright decreed by The High King "to every cow its calf, to every book its copy". The first castle of the O'Conors Sligo was situated at the foot of the mountain in the townland of Castletown of which only a minute fragment exists. A. 15, 19, 194, 377. M. 7, 41, 65, 70, 85, 88, 90, 93, 178, 182, 246. CP. 207, 208, 218, 397, 400. Pl. 641. Ex. 29, 83.

BERA Beare Island, Bantry Bay, County Cork. An Irish expression used to denote from one end of Ireland to the other is "from Malin Head to Mizen Head", but Yeats wrote "from Rachlin to Bera" in 'The Wanderings of Oisin'. The island got its name from legendary Spanish Princess named Beara who married Mogh Nuadhat, the King who compelled Con of the Hundred Battles to divide Ireland into Leth Mogha and Leth Cuinn. C.P. 442.

BERMINGHAM TOWER. See DUBLIN CASTLE. E&I. 362.

BIRDS' MOUNTAIN called Sliabh da-En, the mountain of the two birds by the Four Masters, but now Slieve Daeane, County Sligo, stretches from Ballygawley to Lough Gill, on the summit of which is Loch Dagea, the lake of the two geese, called 'Lough Ia' by Yeats. Ancient monument on the south side of the mountain known as The Cailleach Beare's House. Ballygawley Mountain is the local name for that end of the mountain. M. 79.

BLACK PIG, see VALLEY OF THE BLACK PIG.

BLACK PITTS Blackpits, A small street off Clanbrassil Street, in the Liberties of Dublin City. M. 47.

THE BLASKETS na Blas caodàn. The Blasket Islands off the S.W. extremity of Dingle Peninsula, County Kerry. Dramatic scenery, high cliffs, ruined settlements. Famous for their vast folklore, some of which is preserved in *Western Island* by Robin Flower, *The Islandman* by Tomas O'Crohan, *Twenty Years a-growing* by Maurice O'Sullivan, and the incomparable *Peig*, by one of the last of the traditional Seanachies, Peig Sayers. Now uninhabited. E & I. 324, 325, 327.

BOG OF ALLEN Moin Almhaine, extends over much of the plain of central Ireland : now developed to produce peat (or turf) as fuel. Pl. 30.

BOYNE An Bhoinn. The river Boyne, which figures extensively

in Irish mythology and as a boundary mark in historical times, enters the Irish Sea a few miles from the town of Drogheda. The underworld goddess of the river, Boann and her husband Dagda lived at Bruigh na Boinne, now called New Grange, County Louth. *The Dream of Aenghus.* The traditional source of the Boyne is the spring of segais, the supernatural source of knowledge in The Land of Promise.

The river is usually associated with the Battle of the Boyne (1691) when William of Orange decisively defeated James II. Yeats thought his Butler ancestors fought on the winning side. C.P. 113, M. 349, 401. Pl. 637, 683, 232. E&I. 369. Ex. 349.

BREIFFNY Ancient territory once ruled over by the O'Rorkes, Princes of Breiffny, extending from Lough Gill, County Sligo, through County Leitrim and County Cavan. Later divided into Breiffny O'Rorke (Leitrim) and Breiffny O'Reilly (Cavan). Figures prominently in the history of Ireland up to the middle of the 17th c. The elopement of Dervorgill, wife of Tiernan O'Rorke, with Dermot McMorrow, King of Leinster, made the subject of many stories, plays, ballads, and songs, and the incident alleged to be one possible cause of the Norman invasion of Ireland. M. 199.

BUAL'S HILL The key to the problem of this place name lay in the reference to Caer in "The Old Age of Queen Maeve". The phrase 'his . . . daughter' indicates that Yeats used Bual as the name of the father of Caer. Caer is easily recognised as the young lady over whom Oengus mac in Dagdai (Aonghus an Bhrogha) developed the dread disease of *gradh eagmhaise*, as told in the old story *Aislinge Oenguso*. There (in the edition by Francis Shaw) she is identified as *Caer Ibormeith, ingen Ethail Anbuail a Sid Uamain i crich Connacht* 'Caer Ibormeith, daughter of Ethal Anbuail from Sid Uamain (the fairy mound of Uaman) in the territory of Connacht'. It is evident that Yeats took the second element of the epithet attached to Ethal and thus produced the ghost-name *Bual* for Caer's father and then substituted 'Bual's hill' for Sid Uamain as the location of his supposed dwelling. In Shaw's edition there is an account of how Ailill of Connacht overran Ethal's *sid* in order to persuade him to help in locating Caer for Oengus. This is echoed in Yeats's phrases 'and set them digging under Bual's hill.' The above deduction is confirmed by the previous phrase : 'He replied' is Ailill speaking, as it were, in the person of Oengus.

The meaning of *Anbuail*, as is the case with many such epithets, is unknown. So also is the location of Sid Uamain. This interpretation is confirmed by George Brandon Saul in his *Prolegomena to the study of Yeats's Poems* p. 183 : "Bual's hill" : Caer's father's name was really Etal Anbual (and more than half a dozen earlier printings of the poem read ". . . digging into Anbual's hill"). C.P. 454.

BUCKLEY'S FORD County Sligo. There were two fords over the river Garavogue, one near the Custom House on the Quay, and the second, Buckley's Ford near the entrance of Doorly Park, linking it with the townland of Ardhowen. M. 152, 179.

BURREN County Clare. Boireann, defined in Frost's *History of Clare* (1893) as a rocky district. According to John O'Donovan, the Burren derived its name from 'boor' meaning 'great' or a 'stone'. According to the Dinnseanchus, the word 'Burren' is derived from Boirenn, son of Balcan, son of Ban, who was the son of Illand, who came from Spain. Prior to 10th c. it was known as Corcumruadh Ninnis from the Modruadh Ninnis tribe; their territory was split at a later date into Corcumruadh and Burren.

The O'Daverons, one of the most eminent hereditary legal families in Ireland had a school of Law and History until 17th c. at Cahermacnaghton, the name of one of the many cahers or cashels in the area. At the beginning of the 20th c., the remains of the huts, around the caher in which the students had lived, were still in existence. M. 58. E & I. 209, 211.

BURROUGH Formerly a slum district of Sligo town between the Town Hall and the river Garavogue. The Town Hall is on the site of Sligo Castle which controlled the route from Sligo to Donegal, being near the old ford across the river, so the Burrough probably represented the oldest part of a town, which usually clustered in the vicinity of a castle. No longer known as the Burrough. A. 257. M. 234, 235, 244, 238, 239.

CAILLEAC BUILLIA, Yeats's corruption of Cailleach Beare. See BIRDS' MOUNTAIN. VP. 802.

CAIRNSFOOT Sligo. A secluded house surrounded by nine acres of land lying between St Anne's Church and Sligo Racecourse. M. 71, 72.

CAMDEN STREET HALL Dublin, where the first performance of the Irish National Theatre Society took place. One of the three short plays on the programme was *The Pot of Broth*. The Hall was subsequently used as a workshop making costumes and scenery when the Society moved to the Molesworth Hall. Years later the Hall was used by Countess Markievicz for drilling her boy-scouts. Ex. 86, 100.

CAPPAGHTAGLE Ceapach A' tSeagail, the plot of rye land. A townland in the Barony of Kilconnell, County Galway. M. 222.

CARBURY Coirpre or Cairbre, barony in N. County Sligo, in which are Drumcliff, Rosses, Glencar, Benbulben, Cooladrumman (Cuil Dreimbre); called after Coirpe, the eldest son of Nial of the Nine hostages.

CARA Lough Carra, County Mayo, referred to by George Moore in *The Lake*, but this cannot be the one meant by Yeats in the context of 'Proud Costello', because of its situation.
Lough Gara, where Yeats set the story is almost cut in two, the narrowest part being spanned by a bridge. The upper and smaller part of the lake is known locally as Lough Callow, and 'Carra' may be corruption of 'Callow'. M. 203.

CARRAROE Ceathru Rua, the red quarter, a Gaelic speaking district in Connemara, County Galway, with a popular Irish college. E&I. 337.

CARRICKFERGUS Carraig Fhearghasa, Fergus' Rock, County Antrim, called after Fergus mac Erc, first Irish King of Scotland, who was drowned there. A small port and market town, eleven miles from Belfast. One of the best preserved and most interesting early 13th c. Norman castles in Ireland. Associated also in history with King John, Edward Bruce, William of Orange and Paul Jones. Ruins of old town walls and church. Dean Swift held his first benefice (1694–6) at Kilroot, two miles from Carrickfergus. M. 107.

CARRICK-ORUS Carrickoris, Carraig Fheorais, County Offaly, Bermingham's Rock. The Irish word for Bermingham is Feoris pronounced 'Foris' but as in this case, when preceded by the definite article, it becomes 'Fheoris', pronounced 'Oris'. Carrickoris is on Carrick Hill, three miles from Edenderry. Mainister Fheorais mentioned by the Four Masters (789 A.D.)

Although this is the only place of that name, it is not the place referred to by Yeats in "The Hour Glass". Firstly because he does not refer to any other place in that part of Ireland, secondly, all three places, Kilcluan, Tubber-vanach and Carrick-orus mentioned in that play are near one another and therefore must presumably be in County Galway. Pl. 4, 304.

CASHEL, ROCK OF CASHEL, Caiseal, Cashel of the Steps, Cashel of the Kings, County Tipperary. Cashel is one of the most imposing sites in Ireland. Originally the capital of Munster was in County Kerry, but with the rise of the Eoganacta dynasty it was transferred to Cashel, until Brian Boru again moved it to Kincora, County Clare. Cashel therefore cannot boast the antiquity of Cruachain, Tara, Emain Macha or Ailech, but it possesses fine historic ruins perched on a high acropolis.

At Cashel St Patrick first used the shamrock to explain the doctrine of the Trinity.

The original caiseal was erected in 5th c. probably on the site of an older one, by a King of Munster, making it the capital of Munster. In the 12th c. another King of Munster gave it to the Church. Only Cormac's Chapel and the Round Tower remain. A deeply moving set of ruins.

In 1749 His Grace Archbishop Price had the roof of the cathedral stripped and used to roof a new cathedral on the nearby plain because he could not drive his coach and four up the incline of the Rock, or as Yeats said "no congregation has

26

climbed to the Rock of Cashel since the stout Church of Ireland bishop took the lead roof from the Gothic church to save his legs". C.P. 192, 194. (Ex. 266).

CASHEL-na-GAEL Castlegal, Caisle-Geala, County Sligo, white castle, a townland on the Sligo side of Cope's Mountain. M. 178, 182.

CASHELNORE Alleged by Yeats to be 'near Slieve League', but no such place is known to the inhabitants of that part of County Donegal. There is, however, a Caiseal-an-Oir in Glencomkille, County Donegal which could hardly be described as 'near Slieve League', though it is in sight of it. Sean O'hEochaidh, the folklorist of Gortahort, County Donegal, says that this whole area was an 'Ait uasal' (gentle place) in the old days. M. 86.

CASTLE, THE, DUBLIN CASTLE Before the coming of the Vikings (841) known as Druim-Choll-Coill, hill of the hazel wood. Entrances from Palace Street, off Dame Street, and from Cork Hill. Centre of power in Ireland until 1922. Erected on high ground as the main part of the defences of Dublin 1204–28; four drum towers and gatehouse 14th c.; Bermingham Tower 1411, rebuilt 1775. Largely 18th c. Fine State apartments including Throne Room and St Patrick's Hall which is now used for inaugurations of Presidents and other state functions. Also houses the State Paper Office, the Chapel Royal, the Heraldic Museum and Genealogical Office.

In Yeats's time was synonymous with the Ascendancy, over which the Viceroy presided at social events to which many aspired. A. 233, 430, 566. Pl. 102, 330, 341. E&I. 362.

CASTLE DARGAN Dargan Lake and Castle Dargan Lake. Caiseal-Locha-Deargain, the stone fort of Loch Dargain. Not far from Ballygawley, County Sligo. The ruined castle on the cliff's edge may be the setting for Yeats's play, *Purgatory*. Confirmation of this theory is provided by the true story of a Miss Ormsby of Castledargan who eloped with a groom. They married and lived happily on a small farm in the townland of Glen, between Collooney and Coolaney where their descendants still reside. The play is obviously based on this story. On the side of Slieve Daeane, facing Castledargan, is the house of the Cailleach Beara and on the summit is Lough Dagea – the lake of the two geese, called by Yeats, Lough Ia. A. 53, 54, 55. M. 241, 243, 245. Pl. 640.

CASTLE FURY A big farmhouse in the townland of Ardnabrack, on the edge of Castle Dargan Lake, County Sligo, formerly owned by a family named Furey. Clochmore, a ruined Court Cairn, is on the lands of the farm. About one mile towards Carrownagh crossroads is Cashelore, a stone caiseal of ancient cyclopean stones. Yeats is wrong when he says (A 54) that it is facing Castle Dargan across a lake. It is at the end of the lake. A. 54.

CASTLE HACKETT About three miles from Tuam on the road to Headford, County Galway. Estate of some 900 acres. There was an old castle of the Hacketts of which little remains. Now a mansion which was destroyed by fire in 1923 and restored in 1929. Cnoc-maa is part of this estate. M. 74.

CASTLE HYDE County Cork, on the banks of the river Blackwater. Once O'Mahony property, passed to a Cromwellian family named Hyde, a branch of which produced Douglas Hyde, (An Craoibhin Aoibhinn), Founder of the Gaelic League (1893) and First President of Ireland (1947–49). *Casadh an t-Sugain* (*The Twisting of the Rope*) by him was the first play in Irish performed in a Dublin theatre. A. 217.

CASTLE OF HEROES When Yeats first saw Carraigh Mhic Diarmada with Douglas Hyde, he realised it was the ideal setting for his projected Castle of Heroes. A. 253, 259. See following entry.

CASTLE ROCK and CASTLE ON THE ROCK. Carraig Mhic Diarmada on Loch Cé, County Roscommon. Known by several names such as MacDermots Castle, MacDermots Rock, The Rock, Castle Island. It was the island stronghold of the MacDiarmada, Princes of Maghluirg until after the Williamite Wars.

Gatherings of the artists of Ireland, known as School Invitations, such as were given by many of the Gaelic Chieftains all over Ireland and recorded in *the Annals*, during the 14th and 16th centuries. Two Invitations in the years 1540 and 1549 on Carraig Mhic Diarmada are recorded in *The Annals of Loch Cé*, the existing copy of which was made there for Brian Mac-Diarmada (1588 and 1589) and parts of which are in his handwriting. Yeats dreamed of such a gathering in such a setting.

The Castle was the home of Una Nic Diarmada, heroine of the beautiful Irish love song, 'Una Bhan'. Yeats used a version of the story which is not known to exist elsewhere, in which he places Una's home on the shore of Lough Gara.

When the McDermots' lands were forfeited to Elizabeth I they were then given by her to John King, father of Edward King, about whose death by drowning Milton wrote 'Lycidas'. A. 253, 259.

CASTLE TAYLOR County Galway. Formerly Caislean Mac-Craith of Ballymagrath, near Craughwell. In 1802 the Taylors built a mansion house incorporating the old castle as part of the building. Two of the cut stone gothic windows from one of the seven Churches of Kilmacduagh, were inserted in the Norman keep of Caislean MacCraith, giving it a vulnerability not intended by the builders yet adding a quaint ecclesiastical conceit to a strong fortress. C.P. 150.

CELBRIDGE County Kildare, a small town on the river Liffey. Yeats much admired Castletown House, Celbridge, the largest and finest house (1719–32) in Ireland, and according to him, Bishop Berkeley had been asked by the owner, Speaker Conolly, to help to design the facade; but in reality the house was designed by Allessandro Galilei, a Florentine architect, and Sir Edward Lovett Pearce. It was a living example of the leisured setting Yeats liked. Also, another literary ancestor of Yeats, Jonathan Swift would ride out from Dublin, when Castletown was being built, to visit Esther Vanhomrigh (Vanessa) at her gothic home, Celbridge Abbey. Ex. 349, 431.

CHEVY Chevy Chase, County Galway, the name by which the

townlands of Derrybrien, Daroda and Druim-da-rod in the Echgthe Mountains were known to the Perrse family who owned them. This area has been re-afforested and is now known as Chevy Chase Forest. The name is of Northumbrian origin.

CHURCH ISLAND Inis Mor, the largest and most interesting island on Lough Gill. Ruins of a mediaeval Church on the site of 6th c. monastery.

The O'Cuirnins, hereditary poets to the O'Rorkes of Breiffny, had a school of poetry on this island from the 13th c., and the last members of the family lived there in the middle of the 19th c. Unpublished poems of the last known poet of the family are at Clonalis, Castlerea, Co. Roscommon the home of O'Conor Don.

On this island the *Lebor-na-hUidhre*, the oldest extant book written wholly in Irish, was kept in custody for the O'Conors Sligo, who had been given it in 1359, as ransom by the O'Donnells of Donegal for the return of prisoners of war, until it was later recovered when the fortunes of war changed. Such ransom is not uncommon in Irish history, showing the "meas", or value placed on books by Irish chieftains. The books of the O'Cuirnins including *The Lebor Gerr* were destroyed by fire in 1416. (M. 171.)

CITY HALL Cork Hill, Dublin; built 1769–1779, by Thomas Cooley as the Royal Exchange, but the original building with fine domed Rotunda, has been spoilt by numerous Victorian additions. Taken over by the Corporation 1850. Charters of the City preserved there. Held by the Insurgents in Easter Rising; Connolly, the actor, was the first man to be killed in that Rising. C.P. 373.

THE CLADDAGH in the city of Galway. Originally a distinctive Gaelic village of fisherfolk. Until recent times was an Irish speaking enclave with its own King. The Claddagh ring was the traditional wedding-ring of the whole Irish-speaking coastal district of County Galway. Demolished 1937, replaced by Council houses. Ex. 74.

CLARE An Clar. The stone or the corner of contention. The County of Clare takes its name from a small village of that name, now known as Clarecastle. Before being made a County (1580) it was known as Thomond (Tuadmumu). As the Irish name implies, was originally part of Munster, but later incorporated into Connacht, until it finally reverted to Munster. Stronghold of the Firbolg; home of warriors like Brian Boru and Clare's Dragoons; seat of learning, primarily at Clonmacnois, one of the greatest Schools of The Golden Age where *The Annals of Clonmacnois*, *The Annals of Tighernach* and *The Book of the Dun Cow* were compiled. The oldest copy of *The Children of Lir* (National Library) was made by a County Clare Gaelic scholar named Andrew McCurtain (1680–1740). The electoral constituency of both Daniel O'Connell and Eamon de Valera. A. 401. M. 22, 112. Pl. 98, 435, 439, 647, 667.

CLARE-GALWAY Baile an Chlair, County Galway. The townland of the plain. One of the 15th c. fortified towers with which the de Burgos ringed their territory. Fine ruins of 13th c. Franciscan friary which survived until 1765. Pl. 445.

CLAREMORRIS Clar Chlainne Muiris, the plain of the family of Murris, County Mayo. M. 75.

CLIONA OF THE WAVE Glandore, anciently called Cuandor, golden harbour, County Cork. Cliodhna's Rock in the bay upon which a wave called Tonn-Chliodha beats and is said to wail when a Monarch of the South of Ireland dies. Cliodhna was the name of a fairy princess in an old Irish Legend, sometimes styled Queen of the Munster Fairies. M. 152.

There is a poem on Tonn Chlidna in the 12th c. Dinnshenchus Erenn (The Place-lore of Ireland) said to be uttered by Caoilte in the course of a Colloquy concerning the placelore of Ireland. This Colloquy of Caoilte and Oisin with St. Patrick is set in a journey round Ireland.

CLONDALKIN Cluain Daltain Dallain. Now a suburb of N. Dublin on the road to Naas, once a walled town of the English Pale. Site of the 7th c. monastery. Round Tower. A. 214.

CLONTARF Cluain Tarbh. The meadow of the bulls and Sean Magh Ealta Edair. Old plain of the flocks of Edair. Edair was the name of a chieftain who lived just before the Christian era. Here Brian Boru finally defeated the Vikings (1014) and it must have been the battle referred to by Yeats in *Cathleen ni Houlihan*. Now a suburb of Dublin. Pl. 83. (C.P. 117). E&I. 337. Ex. 8.

CLOONAMAHON Collooney, County Sligo. Cluain-na-Meathan, meadow of the oak slits for sieves. The home of Good Father Hart, of which he was deprived under the Penal laws; now a monastery of the Passionist Order. Thomas O'Conellan, who united the highest skill on the harp with that of a poet, born there in early 17th c. Many of his melodies, introduced to Scotland by his brother Laurence, became popular Scottish airs, such as 'The Battle of Killiekrankie' and 'Farewell to Lochaber', originally, 'Planxty Davis' and 'The Breach of Aughrim.' C.P. 23.

CLOONE BOG County Galway. Two miles from Gort. Originally on the Gregory estate. One of Mary Hynes' admirers accidentally drowned on his way to visit her. M. 26. C.P. 220.

CLOOTH-na-BARE Cailleach Beare. Originally associated with Beare in County Kerry, but like other figures in Irish folklore, extended to many parts of Ireland, notably the megalithic monument on Slieve Daeane not far from Lough Ia in County Sligo, and known as the House of the Cailleach Beare (Berri). M. 79, 237. C.P. 61, 90.

CLOVER HILL Cnoc-na-Seamar County Sligo. The hill of the shamrocks, beside Carrowmore megalithic cemetery, one of the biggest in Europe before the opening of sand pits demolished many of them. There are still 29, all in the shadow of the great Miscaun Maeve of Knocknarea. Pl. 59.

CLOYNE Cluain-Uamha, the meadow of the cave, in *The Book of Leinster*; name of a diocese in County Cork. Also called Cluain Mor. Colman Mac Leneni, founder of the Abbey of

Cloyne, a poet, died in 604, A.D. several fragments of his poems survive. George Berkeley, the philosopher (1685–1753) whose works Yeats much admired was Bishop of Cloyne. C.P. 272.

CNOC-NA-SIDHA Mullach-na-Sidhe, Sidh Aedha Ruaidh (Hugh), Mullaghnashee, Ballyshannon, County Donegal. The dwelling-place of Aed Ruadh, father of Macha, the founder of Emain Macha. He was drowned in the waterfall called after him Eas-Ruadh or Eas-Aedha Ruaidh, sometimes called Cathleen's Falls and anglicised as Assaroe. Conal Gulban is also alleged to have lived there. M. 152.

COLLEGE GREEN Once known as Hoggen Green, then outside the walls of the Norse town of Dublin. Between the bottom of Grafton Street, Dame Street and Westmoreland Street. Flanked by the Palladian facade of Trinity College, outside of which are statues of 'haughtier-headed' Edmund Burke and Oliver Goldsmith 'sipping at the honey-pot of his mind', poses remarked upon by Yeats (C.P. 268). In the centre of the Green, a statue of Thomas Davis the Young Ireland leader (1966). A. 367.

COLOONEY Collooney Cuil Maoile (or Cuil Mhuine) a village in a strategic position in the gap between the Ox Mountains and Slieve Daeane, Co. Sligo. Turlough O'Conor, High King of Ireland, 12th c. built one of the first two fortified castles in Connacht here: the other at Ballinasloe, County Galway. During the Nine Years War (end of the 16th c.) Collooney Castle, at the confluence of the Owenmore and Unchion (or Arrow) rivers, was the last castle in Connacht held for the English by O'Conor, Sligo. One of the few successful engagements of the combined Irish-French forces (1798) was fought at Carricknagat, beside the village of Collooney, where a monument commemorates Bartholomew Teeling, the Irish hero of the day.

Dr O'Rorke, *The History of Sligo; Town and County*. Parish priest of Collooney; Yeats acknowledged his debt to him for several stories, e.g. "The Ballad of Father O'Hart", which is set at Cloonamahon, Collooney. C.P. 24. M. 234, 238, 240, 343.

33

COLUMCILLE'S STRAND Near Drumcliff, County Sligo, no record of the only strand at Drumcliff being called by this name, nor is there any tradition as such in the locality. The origin may have been suggested to Yeats by the lines of the 12th c. poem "Farewell to Ireland" wrongly attributed to the Saint:

> "Beloved also to my heart in the West
> Drumcliff on Culcinne's strand".

The earliest known Irish poem is "Ambra Choluimb Chille", believed to be a 6th c. poem or panegyric by the bard Dallan Forgaill (circa 580), written in old Irish dialect, in gratitude for the Saint's intercession on behalf of the Irish poets at The Convention of Drum Cett (575). M. 92.

COOLANEY Cuil Aine or Cuil Mhaine, County Sligo. A small village five miles W. of Collooney, at the foot of the Ox Mountains, near the pass known as The Hungry Rock. A short distance on the right hand side near the summit is a conspicuous rock known as Carraig an Seabhac – The Hawk's Rock – which in turn is equally near to Tullaghan Holy Well, called by Yeats The Hawk's Well.

About 100 yards from Coolaney bridge, a road to the right leads to another pass through the Ox Mountains passing Hart's Lake, and the Heart Lake (Lough Achree) at the foot of the Ladies Brae, at the other end of the pass to the Sligo-Ballina road.

There is no lake at Coolaney or one known by that name. Pl. 63, 65, 72.

COOL-A-VIN Coolavin, Cuil O'bhFinn, the corner of the territory of Finn, a son of Fergus Mac Roy, ancestor of the tribe called Dal Coufinn, later O'Finn. On the border of County Sligo and County Roscommon adjoining Lough Gara (formerly Lough Techet). Owned by the O'Gara family until the Mac Dermots of Moylurg took up residence there when they lost their lands at Lough Key. They built a house at Sroove on the shore of Lough Gara, and The MacDermot became known as The Prince of Coolavin. This is the setting erroneously given by Yeats as the home of Una NicDermot in 'Proud Costello'.

Afterwards the family moved to a newer house in Coolavin, the entrance to which is opposite Toberaraght, St Attracta's Well, also known as Clogher Well. A fine restored cashel in the grounds. The Barony of Coolavin is closely associated with St Attracta, who received the veil from St Patrick and maintained a Hospital or house of hospitality for travellers at Killaraght.

Fergal O'Gara, 17th c. chieftain of Moygara in the Barony of Coolavin, financed the authors of *The Annals of the Four Masters* (1632–1636) M. 197, 199. Pl. 645.

COOLE Coole Park; an cúil, the corner or nook, near Gort, County Galway. The estate was purchased in 1768 by Robert Gregory who was born in Galway city and made money as Director of the East India Company. Thereafter successive generations of Gregorys lived there until Sir William Gregory, the Governor of Ceylon and husband of Augusta Gregory. In 1892 she had been widowed and then she devoted the second half of her life to making Coole a place where the greatest writers in Ireland could meet and talk, or, as in the case of Yeats, have peace in which to work. The house was typically Irish, neither grand nor imposing but a simple cube of six bays on the east front, with a Palladian window in the centre. In its setting of open parkland it had a sturdy plainness which did not give the impression it had been built for defence like so many Irish houses. Its treasures included a fine library started in the 18th c.

Coole Park meant more to Yeats than any other house in his life. In 1898 he was physically sick, poor and homeless : Augusta Gregory nursed him back to health, lent him money and gave him ideal conditions in which to work. 'I found at last', he wrote, 'what I had been seeking always, a life of order, and of labour, where all outward things were the image of an inward life.' One finds in his work written over a period of thirty years, much of the imagery inspired by living at Coole : the wild swans, the Seven Woods and above all his admiration for Lady Gregory, for Coole was her creation in which she could write her own plays, diaries and stories, as well as being a centre for literary meetings.

In 1927 it was sold to the Ministry of Lands and Agriculture though Lady Gregory was allowed to live there during her lifetime. Five years later she died aged eighty. In 1941 Coole was again sold, to a building contractor who pulled it down for the value of the stone. Nothing remains but the garden walls, the ruins of the stable block and a few floor tiles from the hall. The Autograph Tree, an old copper beech on which famous visitors had been invited to inscribe their initials, remains, now protected by an iron fence, though too late to have prevented desecration. Efforts have been made to restore the garden to something resembling its original state. V. 9, 17, 221. A. 377, 378, 380, 381, 385, 388, 395, 401, 438, 455, 500, 502, 509. E & I. 518. Ex. 318, 319. C.P. 27, 275.

CONNACHT Coicid Connacht, Connachta, Fifth of Connacht, one of the Five Fifths of Ireland, sometimes called Olneamacht. Ruled from Cruachain. According to legend, the Firbolgs divided Ireland into five parts, later to be known as provinces, of which Connacht was one. The word 'Coicid' meaning one fifth, was given to each division and continued in use even though the number of provinces varied from four to six.

There are two origins given for its derivation. The first that Connachta, is a collective noun to denote the descendants of Conn of The Hundred Battles who ruled there; the other, that it was named after a tribe, called Olnechacht, aboriginal settlers in the province, or Olnecm acta. It is thought that this is the origin of the name 'Nagatae' given by Ptolemy to a district in Connacht which some scholars place at Sligo. A. 70, 80, 137. C.P. 306. M. 20, 22, 67, 213, 236. Pl. 224, 228, 235, 645, 658, 659, 664, 676, 695. Ex. 90, 93, 113, 193. E & I. 4, 271, 349.

CONNEMARA Conmaicne-Mara, County Galway. Derived from the descendants of Conmac, one of the sons of Maeve and Fergus Mac Roy, known as Conmaicne. One branch became known as Conmaicne-Mara, the hound sons of the sea, because the western border of their territory is the Atlantic coast. Also known as Iar Connacht, (Western Connacht). One of the isolated areas in Ireland in which the Gaelic heritage survived longest in the district known as the Gaeltacht. A. 361. C.P. 51, 166. M. 226. Pl. 443. E & I. 350.

COPE'S MOUNTAIN Mountain on the S. side of Glencar Valley with Lugnagall on the valley side of it and Cashel-na-Gael, now Castlegal townland, on the opposite or Sligo town side. M. 31, 85.

CORCOMROE ABBEY Corcomruadh, four miles E. of Bally-vaghan, County Clare. (Although written Corcomroe, it is locally pronounced 'Corcumrua'). Derived its name from Modhruadh, son of Maeve by Fergus Mac Roy, whose progeny became known as Corca Modhruadh, (the children of Modhruadh).

Abbey was founded in 1182 by Donal Mor O'Brien, King of Munster for the Cistercians, and called The Abbey of St Mary of the Fertile Rock. Very fine ruin and a superb setting for *The Dreaming of the Bones*. About 4 miles off is Vernon Lodge, the seaside house of the Gregorys of Coole and where Yeats, Bernard Shaw and other literary friends visited Lady Gregory. Pl. 434, 439.

CORK Coraigh, a marsh, County Cork. The third largest city in Ireland, where St Finnbarr founded a monastery in the 7th c. on the site of the present cathedral. From the Vikings to the present day Cork has been the scene of continual struggles for possession because of its strategic position in controlling the province of Munster. Sacked by Vikings, Normans, Cromwell and William of Orange. University College, founded 1845, now part of the National University of Ireland. Home of many distinguished writers including Thomas Crofton Croker, Daniel Corkery, Sean O'Faolain, and Frank O'Connor. A. 227, 409. M. 48. B. 21, 27. Ex. 75, 98. E & I. 46.

COUNTRY-UNDER-WAVE Tir-Fa-Tonn. When the Tuatha de Danann were defeated, they retired to islands, fairy mounds and under-water places. The latter were referred to as Tir-fa-tonn, anglicised as Country under the Wave. Pl. 28, 258, 268, 269, 290. Ex. 23.

CRAGLEE See GREY ROCK. Ex. 283, 285, 286.

CREVROE Craobh-ruadh – the building at Emain Macha in which the Knights of the Red Branch lived. The name is perpetuated in the present townland of Creeveroe, County Armagh. C.P. 444.

CRO-PATRICK, CROAGH PATRICK, Cruach Phadraig near Westport, Clew Bay, County Mayo. Popularly called 'The Reek'. St Patrick is alleged to have fasted on the summit (441ft.) and while there banished serpents from Ireland. An annual pilgrimage to the summit, on which there is a small church, on Garland Sunday (the last Sunday in July) called Lugnasa. The pilgrimage known as 'Climbing the Reek'. A. 194. C.P. 304, 305. Pl. 20. Ex. 266. E. & I. 236.

CRUACHAIN, see CRUACHAN

CRUACHAN Cruacha, Uaimh Cruacha. An older name is Druim-na-nDriaidh, the ridge of the druids. Near the village of Tulsk, County Roscommon. Called after Maeve's mother, Cruacha. The fabled capital of Connacht from pre-Christian times. Featured in many of the sagas and stories of ancient Ireland, notably in *The Táin Bó Cuailnge*; the beginning and end of that book occur there, with the respective mounds of Rath Cruachan and Rath na DTarbh in close proximity and still identifiable. The site of the pagan Aenach Connacta.

One of the oldest royal sites and burial grounds, Relig na Riogh – where many of the early legendary heroes and heroines of Ireland are alleged to be buried. On the edge of the cemetery is a Red Standing Stone, marking the spot where Daithi, the last pagan High King of Ireland, is buried. Also the probable burial place of Maeve.

Near the cemetery is the cave referred to as the mouth of the underworld, with an Ogham inscription on one of the roofing stones; known locally as 'Maeve's Treasury'. This underworld cave features in an old tale "Echtra Nerai", ("The Adventures of Nera".)

Cruachan covers an extensive area resembling a military encampment, originally having five concentric circles of forts dominated at the apex by Rath Cruachain. Many of the forts survive, as well as short sections of the old road leading from Tara to Cruachain.

Between Cruachan and the village of Tulsk is The Well of Ogulla or The Well of Clebach, where St Patrick baptised Eithne the Fair and Fedelma the Ruddy, two daughters of Laoghaire, the High King of Ireland. C.P. 130, 304, 305, 306, 451, 453. V. 28. Pl. 255. Ex. 13, 17, 136.

CRUACHMAA Knockmaa, a hill on Castle Hackett estate three miles from Tuam, County Galway. Most writers say the word is derived from Maeve but Stephen Gwynn, *The Fair Hills of Ireland* attributes it to Cnoc-maighe, the hill of the plain, which is the more likely as it is alleged to be the underworld dwelling of Finnvarra, King of the Fairies of Connacht and is unlikely to be associated with Maeve. Secondly, it is a hill on a plain. M. 152. V. 28. E. & I. 211, 212, 295.

CUMMEN Cuimín, the little common, County Sligo. The townland and strand are on the road from Sligo to Strandhill. A line of bollards from the strand to Coney Island indicates the pedestrian route to the island when the tide is out. M. 237. C.P. 61.

CURRAGH County Kildare, usually applied to a flat or level terrain such as the Curragh between Carraroe and Belladrihid, County Sligo. The Curragh of Kildare referred to, is synonymous with horse-racing. Today also the site of the largest Irish military establishment and the Curragh jail or internment camp. Pl. 683.

DAOIRE-CAOL County Galway. The narrow oak wood. Correctly Daire-vo-Caol; currently Derry-vo-Keel. In Slieve Echgthe. M. 222.

DEAD MAN'S POINT County Sligo. The extremity of the land at Rosses Point, County Sligo, between the Channel (the tidal part of the Garavogue) and the Strand of Rosses Point. Maritime extremity of the strip of land on which Elsinore and The Pilot House are built. M. 191.

39

DERRY Doire, the oak grove, on the river Foyle, County Derry; called Derry in Ireland, but Londonderry outside of Ireland. The latter name dates from the granting of the city and large tracts of lands by James I to the citizens of London, when it was planted with Protestant settlers.

The origin dates back to a monastery founded by St Columcille (546). It suffered the usual attacks by Viking raiders; but its most memorable event was the siege in 1689 during the Williamite War. The closing of the gates in the city walls by the Apprentice Boys is still commemorated annually. The city walls are the best preserved in Ireland or England.

Five miles from Derry, or Derry Columcille as it was sometimes called, is the impressive Grianan Aileach, shown on Ptolemy's 1st c. map of Ireland as Aileach Ned, the capital of Ulster after the destruction of Emain Macha. Ex. 348.

DERRYBRIEN County Galway, Daire Bhriain, Brian's oak wood. Slieve Echgthe. Source of Abhain da Loilgheach, the river of the two milk cows, belonging to the Lady Echgthe, from whom the mountain takes its name; referred to in the legend of the origin of the name 'Echgthe' as told by the poet, Flan Mac Lonan, the 'Virgil of the race of Scota, who died in 892' (FM). M. 26.

DINGLE BAY An Daingean, the fortress, County Kerry. Situated beside Dingle Bay on the Dingle Peninsula and overlooked by Slieve Mish, associated with many mythological heroes. The peninsula rich in megalithic and early historic remains. Irish speaking enclaves in the peninsula. E. & I. 337.

DIRTY LANE Dublin, now known as Bridgefoot Street joining Thomas Street with the Liffey, opposite St Catherine's church, Dublin. M. 50.

DONEGAL Dun-na-nGall, the fort of the strangers, County Donegal, formerly called Tir Conaill. Tirconnell, the country of the progeny of Connell or Conal, the son of Nial of the Nine Hostages who was fostered at Benbulben. Prior to the O'Donnell ascendancy (10th c.) it was the territory of the O'Canannains.

The O'Donnells and the O'Neills represent the Northern Branch of the Ui Neill who gave seven High Kings to Ireland. The magnificent stone fort of Ailech or Ailech Ned, named as such by Ptolemy, was their chief stronghold. Columcille was a member of the family which provided many notable Irishmen and women including the heroic Red Hugh O'Donnell. His sister Nuala is the subject of the magnificent early 17th c. Gaelic poem by Eoghan Ruadh Mac an Bhaird in *The Book of O'Donnell's Daughter* and translated by James Clarence Mangan, as "The Lament for the Princes".

The O'Donnells were great patrons of the arts and benefactors of the Church. Their history is enshrined in the many ruins in Donegal. A. 50, 123, 217. M. 77, 83, 84. E & I. 486. Pl. 37.

DONERAILE Dun-air-Aill, the fort on the cliff, County Cork. Originally a Desmond stronghold granted with over 3,000 acres to Edmund Spenser circa 1587.

Sir Walter Raleigh visited Spenser at Kilcolman in 1589. Canon Sheehan, a very popular novelist in Ireland at the end of the 19th c., was parish priest of Doneraile, where most of his novels were written. A. 401. Ex. 69. E & I. 515. V. 221.

DONN OF THE VATS OF THE SEA Teach Dhuinn or Donn's House, three rocks in Kenmare Bay, County Kerry, where Donn, one of the Milesian brothers was drowned; rocks are now known as Bull, Cow, and Calf. Mentioned in *The Children of Lir*. M. 152.

DOONEY ROCK County Sligo, Dun Aodh, Aodh's (Hugh's) fort. On the shores of Lough Gill, magnificent view from the top of the rock.

In Yeats' time the Rock was a meeting place for outdoor country dances on Sunday evenings, when the music was supplied by James Howley, a blind fiddler from Ballysadare. A. 377. C.P. 82.

DORREN'S ISLAND County Sligo. Now known as Coney Island, Inis Cuinin, from a story connected with St Patrick.

It was known formerly as Dorren's Island, lying between Kilaspugbrone and Rosses Point, accessible at ebb tide on foot or by car from Cummen Strand. M. 191.

DOWN, An Dun. Old name for Downpatrick, County Down, was Dun-Da-Leth-glas, the fort of the two broken fetters; the name later shortened to Dun and given to the County of that name. The Dal Fiatach, Kings of Ulaid, were inaugurated at Creeb Tulcha in the north of Co. Down. After the destruction of Emain Macha (451) Ulaid was confined to E. County Down.

Yeats' grandfather was Rector of Moira, County Down. A. 34, 53.

DRIM-na-ROD Druim-Da-Rod, County Galway. The ridge of the two roads. In Sliabh Echgthe. The usual Irish word for road is 'bothar', but 'rod' (pronounced 'road') is another Irish word for road. One of the resting places of Diarmuid and Grainne. Lady Gregory says that Derrybrien, Drum-da-rod and Daroda (the two roads) were all referred to by the Persses as Chevy Chase. M. 222. E. & I. 77.

DROMAHAIR Dromahaire, County Leitrim. Drom-Dha-Eithiar, the ridge of the two demons. The village of Dromahaire is on the river Bonnet which flows into the County Leitrim end of Lough Gill. The stronghold of the O'Rorkes of Breiffny, chiefly remembered as the place that Dervorgilla, daughter and sister of Kings of Meath, wife of O'Rorke, King of Breiffny, eloped (1151) with Dermot MacMorrough, King of Leinster, but soon after retired to the Monastery of Mellifont where she lived a devout life for many years. Legend, if not history, blames her elopement for the Norman Invasion. Beside the river bank near Lough Gill, part of one gable of the castle from which she eloped is still standing. The shell of O'Rorke's Banqueting Hall is also by the river in the village. Used by Swift in the poem "The Description of an Irish Feast" translated almost literally out of the original Irish (1720).

O'Rorke's Table, a remarkable conical hill, the meeting place of the clansmen, is a few miles from the village.

Crevelea Abbey, An Chraobh Liath, the Grey branch, founded 1508 by the O'Rorkes, is a fine ruined Franciscan friary. M. 5, 70. C.P. 49.

DRUMCLIFF Druim-Chliach, the ridge of the hazels, County Sligo, at the foot of Ben Bulben on the Drumcliff river, near the mouth of Glencar valley.

St Columcille founded a monastery here in 575 of which there is now no trace; but there is the lower part of a Round Tower, a fine High Cross with scenes from the Scriptures, and the shaft of an older Cross in the wall of the church yard where the poet is buried. The dualism of the mythology of Ireland, Christian and pagan, is here centred. So it was Yeats's wish to be buried near the church, though the proud epitaph is unusually pagan. Here he would join his ancestors and the heroic figures of Irish legend.

On the opposite side of the road nearer the bridge is a three-storeyed Rectory where the poet's grandfather lived. A. 19. C.P. 370, 400. M. 5, 70, 88, 92, 93, 94.

DRUMCONDRA Drom Chonnrach, the ridge of the path. Modern suburb of N. Dublin on main Belfast Road; St Patrick's Training College for National School Teachers and All Hallowes College on the site of an Augustinian Friary, founded by Dermot McMorrough, King of Leinster in 1163. A.368.

DUBLIN Baile Atha Cliath, the ford of the hurdles, the capital of Ireland. Called Eblana by Ptolemy. Where the Vikings built a walled town, Dubhlinn(a black pool); were defeated by Brian Boru (11th c.) Never a Gaelic city. Centre of English government from Henry II (Strongbow) until 1922. Lowest ebb in Cromwellian times; thereafter changed from a medieval town into a metropolis regarded as the second city in the British Empire. Such buildings as Sir Edward Lovett Pearce's Parliament House, now the Bank of Ireland, and later James Gandon's Custom House and Four Courts, as well as elegant streets and squares. Yeats much admired these and lived with his family, 1922–28, at 82 Merrion Square, one of the most handsome. Extreme poverty of the working classes in the early 19th c. and particularly during the Great Famine (1845–9) when starving refugees poured in. At the end of the 19th c. was the centre of the national cultural revival of which Yeats was one of the leaders. Much damaged during the Easter Rising (1916) and the Civil War (1922–23). See FOUR COURTS and POST OFFICE.

Yeats, descended from Dublin merchants, born and educated in Dublin himself. It was the birthplace of the following mentioned by Yeats: Jonathan Swift, Edmund Burke, Richard Brinsley Sheridan, Tom Moore, James Clarence Mangan, Wolfe Tone, Oscar Wilde, G. B. Shaw and James Joyce. A. 22, 85, 86, 96, 116, 117. M. 20, 267. C.P. 113. B. 21, 32. V. 19.

DUBLIN ART SCHOOLS, see ARTS SCHOOLS.

DUBLIN CASTLE, see CASTLE, THE.

DUBLIN MUNICIPAL GALLERY See MUNICIPAL GALLERY OF MODERN ART. C.P. 238. E & I. 343.

DUNBOY, uncertain. M.15.

DUNDALK, see DUNDEALGAN. E & I. 335.

DUNDEALGAN Now Dundalk in County Louth. Originally called Straidbhaile, beside Traghbaile, also Baile na Tragha (Baile's Strand) 'Dun Dealgan' derived from a prehistoric fort alleged to be the home of Cuchulain. One of the outposts of the English Pale and as such the scene of many military engagements. Edward Bruce crowned King of Ireland at Knocknamelan just outside Dundalk where he was buried. Pl. 247.

DURAS Dubh-ros, the dark promontory, County Clare, between Kinvara Bay and Aughanish Bay. The home of Comte Florimond de Basterot, the friend of Lady Gregory; where the idea of a Literary Theatre was born. Now a Youth Hostel. A. 380, 397. M. 28. Pl. 117, 118.

EADES GRAMMAR SCHOOL The Mall, Sligo. Opened 1907, prior to that date the old Diocesan School (Protestant) was the

Erasmus Smith (17th c.) foundation at Primrose Grange on the Glen side of Knocknarea. Originally for boys, now a Comprehensive School. Yeats refers to it as 'Eade's grammar school' because the headmaster at that time was named Eade. C.P. 176.

ECHTGE Sliabh Echgthe, now Slieve Aughty, sometimes referred to as Slieve Baughty, a range of mountains stretching from Loughrea in County Galway to near Lough Derg on the Shannon in County Clare.

The mountain got its name from Echgthe a De Danann Lady who was given it as her marriage dowry to graze her herds of cattle. From there a river, rising in the Derrybrien townland, got the name Abhainn-da-Loingheach – the river of the two milch cows – anglicised Owendalulagh River.

At the beginning of 20th c. it contained a number of villages or hamlets, in which Irish was spoken and the native oral tradition still prevalent. Yeats and Lady Gregory enumerate many villages with variations in spelling, and Lady Gregory in her *Seventy Years* acknowledges her debt to the inhabitants for much of her folklore in *Visions and Beliefs in the West of Ireland"*. Ex. 40. E. & I. 77, 211. M. 26, 220, 222, 229, 232, 253. C.P. 87, 88.

ELSINORE Elsinore Lodge, the summer residence of William Middleton, grand-uncle of the poet, at Rosses Point, looking out on the Channel to Sligo Quay. (For Middleton's other house, see AVENA). C.P. 372.

ELY PLACE a fine, short, Georgian cul-de-sac at the end of Merrion Street, Dublin. Named after the Earl of Ely who built No 8, Ely House, which has some of the finest plaster-work in Dublin (1770). Often visited by the poet, in company with George Russell, Maud Gonne and others for meetings of the Dublin Theosophical Society. A. 236, 249.

EMAIN, EMAIN MACHA, Macha's Height now Navan Fort, two miles from Armagh town, Capitail of Ulaid. Founded by Macha, Queen of Ulaid, who defined its circumference by marking a track in the ground with the point of her brooch, enclosing eighteen acres. Ptolemy marked it on his map of Ireland as

Isamnion. Its epoch lasted from the 3rd c. B.C. to 450 A.D. Its greatest glory was in the time of Conor Mac Nessa and the Red Branch Knights. The Heroic Age in Ireland ends with the destruction of Emain Macha by the Three Collas.

Niall O'Neill momentarily revived some of its glory in 1381 when he entertained the poets of Ireland there as the O'Carrolls, O'Kellys and MacDermots did in other parts of Ireland. C.P. 17, 459. Pl. 695. Ex. 29.

ENNISCRONE Inis Crabhann, the promontory of Crone, called Inis Sgrebhoinn and Eisker Abhainn in old MSS. A seaside village in County Sligo, five miles from Ballina. Legend of a mermaid who married an O'Dowd, King of North Connacht, and later returned to the sea after changing her seven children into seven pillar stones known as the Children of the Mermaid. Pl. 78, 82.

ESSERKELLY County Galway, Esirtkelly, Dysert Cheallagh or Disert Ceallagh, Ceallagh's Hermitage after St. Ceallagh (F.M.,) Near Ardrahan, County Galway. He was the eldest son of Eoghan (Owen) Bel, the last pagan King of Connacht, who was killed in the battle of Sligo and is the most likely person to be buried under Miscaun Maeve on Knocknarea. C.P.'150.

ESSEX BRIDGE Over the Liffey, Dublin, called after the Earl of Essex, the favourite of Elizabeth I. Now known as Grattan Bridge, but often called Capel Street bridge by Dubliners, because it joins Capel Street with Parliament Street. M. 50, 51.

ESS RUADH, Eas Rua, Ballyshannon, County Donegal. The waterfall or cataract of Aodh Ruadh, the father of Macha, the founder of Emain Macha, who lived beside it in Síd Aedha, anglicised Mullaghasee, as Eas Ruadh is Assaroe. Legend says that Finn Mac Cumhaill liked to slumber to the sound of the falling water here. A. 458.

FADDLE ALLEY Near St. Patrick's Cathedral, Dublin. Now Dowker's Lane linking Clanbrassil Street with Blackpits. Zosimus, the blind balladeer, was born here. Many of the streets and lanes of the Liberties preserved by Zosimus in his ballads. He ("Michael Moran") is the subject of "The Last Gleeman" in *Mythologies*. M. 47.

FAIR HEAD Beann Mhor, the big peak, County Antrim. Nearby, Carraig Uisneach associated with Deirdre and the Sons of Uisneach (Usna). An old ruin called 'The Goban Saor's Castle' is near. Pl. 30.

FINVARA (written, and pronounced 'Finievara'), Fidh an Mhara, the wood by the sea. A rocky promontory on the coast of N. County Clare. Site of a celebrated school of poetry under the family of O'Dalaigh (O'Daly), hereditary poets to the O'Loughlins in medieval times. The family of O'Dalaigh, the most renowned family of these poets in Ireland, among whom Donnchadh Mor O'Dalaigh of the Cistercian Abbey of Boyle was the greatest religious and nature poet in Ireland in the 13th c. In the 17th c. Cearbhall O'Dalaigh composed the song 'Eibhlin a Ruin' (Eileen Aroon), which Yeats heard sung at Kiltartan crossroads. Pl. 435.

FIRBOLGS' BURIAL MOUNDS County Sligo. In "The Wanderings of Oisin", is Carrowmore. Ceathru-mor, the big quarter, between Sligo and Knocknarea, the site of one of the biggest megalithic burial grounds in Europe. Thought to be the burial ground of the Firbolgs defeated at the Battle of Moytirra. In the middle of the 19th c. John O'Donovan counted about 160 graves, today there are only 29. C.P. 409.

FLUDDY'S LANE Not traceable. "In the village of H——, in Leinster". M. 19.

FOUR COURTS Courts of Law at Inns Quay, Dublin. Architect, James Gandon who built a majestic building (1786–96), with a domed central mass. Occupied by Volunteers, Easter 1916, but suffered little damage. In the Civil War, the Insurgents blew up much by explosives, including the Public Record Office and the Law Library : an irreparable loss. Reconstruction undertaken 1932, little of Gandon's building left. M. 303.

GABHRA In "The Wanderings of Oisin", Yeats refers to Gabhra's raven-covered plain. There were three battles of Gabhra at different places and times but the one indicated here is obviously that near Garristown, County Dublin at which the Fianna were almost exterminated (281) C.P. 410.

GABHRA LOUGH Loch Gabhair near Dunshaughlin, County Meath, now known as Lagore. There was a crannog on the lake which was the headquarters of the Kings of Bregia and therefore an important place.

In 'Proud Costello', Yeats refers to Lough Gabhra in the belief that this is the Irish name of Lough Gara partly in County Sligo and partly in County Roscommon, where the story is set. See CARA. There is no Lough Gabhra in Connacht. The old name for Lough Gara is Loch Techet. McDermot's latter day house was at Sroove on the shore of Lough Gara. M. 155, 203, 204, 208.

GALWAY County Galway, Cathair na Gaillimh, the City of Galway, the Citie of the Tribes – from its ruling oligarchy of fourteen merchant families. Important market centre, university and cathedral town. Long a trading port with Spain, as Yeats notes (C.P. 113); isolated from English power.

Duald Mac Firbis (1585–1670) author of *The Book of Genealogies of Ireland*; Dr John Lynch, (1599–1673) author of *Cambrensis Eversus* and Roderick O'Flaherty, (1629–1718) author of *Ogygia*.

Galway Races an all-Ireland event which Yeats uses to show his dislike of middle-class clerks etc. as compared with those who ride horses. (C.P. 108) A. 150, 217, 369, 385, 391, 392, 453. C.P. 108, 113. M. 9, 44, 112. Pl. 82, 443. B. 10, 11. Ex. 31, 50, 52, 89, 134, 231, 235, 240, 402, 412. E & I. 90, 97, 211, 517, 340. V. 227, 301.

GAP OF THE WIND See WINDY GAP.

GEESALA ,Gwesala, Gaoh Saile, the sea or salt breeze. A small Irish speaking village on Blacksod Bay, Co. Mayo. E & I. 337.

GLASNEVIN Glas-Naeidhen, Naeidhe's little stream, Dublin. St. Moibhi founded a monastery here (6th c.) at which St. Columcille studied, and which became one of the most famous of Irish monasteries.

Glasnevin Cemetery, the principal burial-ground for Dublin since 1831. The following, mentioned by Yeats, are buried here : Daniel O'Connell (1775–1847), James Clarence Mangan (1803–41), Charles Stewart Parnell (1846–91), Sir Roger Casement (1864–1916), Countess Markievicz (1868–1927), Arthur Griffith (1872–1922) and Michael Collins (1890–1922). C.P. 123, 319.

GLEN County Sligo, Cochrane of the Glen, on the N. side of Knocknarea. A remarkable chasm giving the effect of a roofless cathedral. Has an unusually mild climate and formerly a variety of tropical and semi-tropical plants brought there by the Phibbs family of Lisheen. Cochrane lived at Glen Lodge, Cullenamore in the grounds of which the Glen is situated. The Glen is also referred to by Yeats as 'Alt'. A. 284. C.P. 393.

GLEN-CAR, GLENCAR, GLENCAR LOUGH. An Chairthe, Gleann an Chairthe. The Glen of the standing stone, County Sligo. Glencar is locked between Benbulben and Cope's Mountain (Slievemore). The lake once held a strategic crannog, the scene of numerous sieges and intrigues. An outpost of the O'Rorkes of Breffny. Several waterfalls, the biggest of which Yeats wrote of; but the most fascinating is that known as Sruth-in-naghaidh-an-Aird, the stream against the cliff, from the water being blown backward like a veil. He refers to it, but not by name in 'Towards Break of Day' (C.P. 208). M. 158. C.P. 21.

GLENDALOUGH, Glen-da-Locha. The valley glen of the two lakes, wooded country one mile W. of Laragh, County Wicklow, famous for its scenic beauty and for the ruins of a monastic school that flourished there. The monastery, originating with the hermitage of St. Kevin, (died 618) in 7th c. grew until it became one of the greatest monastic schools in Ireland and a place of pilgrimage. St. Kevin's bed is a small cave in the rock 30 feet above the waters of the Upper Lake. The ruined churches, crosses and Round Tower are placed in a site ringed by mountains in a setting of great beauty. C.P. 154, 288. Pl. 350. V. 9.

GOBAN'S MOUNTAIN-TOP Sliabh Anieran, now Slieve Anieran, the iron mountain, County Leitrim. Goibhniu, the God of the smiths, helped make and repair the weapons of war on this mountain for the Tuatha de Danann who had landed in a mist on it before the Battle of Moytirra. In the 6th or 7th c. the god appears in Irish literature as Gobhan Saer, Gobhan the wright, a great architect alleged to be the builder of many ancient monuments, the ruins of which are scattered over the country. Today the term "gobbaun" is used as a derisory one for an unskilled tradesman. M. 66. C.P. 115, 119, 131.

GORT Gort, Innse-Guaire, the island field of Guaire, a small, well-planned marked town. A 6th c. King of Connacht was visited here by Senchen Torpest, Chief Poet of Ireland, with a retinue of 150 poets, 150 pupils, servants and followers. He stayed for one year, one quarter and one month. It was he who called a meeting of the Fili to take steps to recover the lost work known as *Cuilmenn Bo Chuailgne*. The miraculous recovery is related in Cormac's *Glossary* and by O'Curry and Ferguson, and how Senchen called up Fergus Mac Roy from the grave to recite it. Senchen is the author of a historical poem preserved in *The Book of Lecan* and is the hero of *The King's Threshold*. Two miles N. is the entrance to Coole Park. See COOLE. A. 392, 425. M. 65, 112, 117. C.P. 214. Pl. 107, 110, 116. Ex. 102. E & I. 233.

GORTIN Gurteen, Gortin, little tilled field, in the parish of Kilbecanty (pronounced Kilbaycanty) County Galway. A common name throughout Ireland. M. 122.

GRANAGH Grannach, a sandy place, townland near Ardrahan, County Galway. M. 219.

GRANGE Grainseach County Sligo, near Benbulben and Streedagh Strand. Grange is the name given to any townland where great mediaeval monasteries stored grain. In County Sligo, Grange and Primrose Grange, on the side of Knocknarea, belonged to Cistercian Abbey, Boyle. M. 7.

GREEN LANDS The Greenlands. The unfenced part of Rosses Point from Deadman's Point inland, the highest point of which is known as Bearnais Aird. Yeats used to walk over these desolate sandhills with George Pollexfen, as also did Henry Middleton 'every Sunday afternoon'. M. 243. C.P. 372.

GRESHAM HOTEL O'Connell Street, Dublin, formerly Sackville Street. Founded in 1817 by an Englishman named Gresham who rose from poverty to become Lord Mayor of London. One of Dublin's principal hotels; was demolished during the Civil War (1922). Rebuilt and reopened in 1927. A favourite meeting place of members of the old Nationalist Party. A. 256.

GREY ROCK and CRAGLEE Craig Liath, grey stone, a striking rock of 40 feet, one mile from Killaloe, County Clare, celebrated in Irish fairy lore as the house of Aoibheal, the banshee of the Dal Cais tribe. A well named after her is nearby. Yeats refers to the banshee as Aoibheal (M. 152) Aoibhell (Ex. 8) Eevell (Ex. 283, 285) and as Aoife (C.P. 118). M. 152. C.P. 115. Ex. 8, 283, 285, 286.

GURTEEN DHAS Dundrum, Dublin, was the home of Susan Mary (Lily) and Elizabeth (Lollie) Yeats' sisters. A. 515.

HARCOURT STREET SCHOOL No. 40, Harcourt Street, off Stephen's Green, Dublin, an Erasmus Smith foundation where Yeats went to school (1880–1884). A. 56, 79.

HAROLD'S CROSS Suburb of S. Dublin where John B. Yeats lived with his family briefly at No 142 Harold's Cross Road. Venue of greyhound racing, frequented by Cornelius Patterson in *The Words upon the Window Pane*. Thomas Davis, Young Ireland poet, and Edmund Dowden buried in St. Jerome Cemetery at Harold's Cross. Pl. 599.

HART LAKE County Sligo. A small, 'drear' lake at the summit of the Ox Mountains on the pass from Coolaney to Skreen. The lake takes this contemporary name from the family of Hart living beside it. In older documents and maps it is Loch Minnaun. C.P. 63. E & I. 26.

HAWK'S WELL County Sligo. Otherwise Tullaghan Well or St. Patrick's Well, in the townland of Tullaghan about one mile from Coolaney village, on the side of the Ox Mountains. Listed as one of the Mirabilia Hibernia of Ireland by Nennius, Giraldus Cambrensis and O'Flaherty, the reason being that although the range of the Ox Mountains lies between it and the sea, the water in it ebbs and flows with the tide. There is a legend that the well sprang up at the prayer of St. Patrick, after whom it was called.

Carraig-an-Seabhach, The Hawk's Rock, a striking rock lies between the well and the main range of the Ox Mountains. Pl. 207, (292), 699.

HEART LAKE Loch Achree, County Sligo. Known as the youngest lake in Ireland; the Four Masters record its appearance as the result of an earthquake in 1490. At the foot of The Ladies Brae at the Skreen end of the pass through the Ox Mountains to Coolaney. The name has two attributions : firstly, it is heart-shaped, and secondly there is a local story of drowning, after which the heart of a horse was seen floating on the lake. M. 73, 76.

HELL MOUTH a cave near Cruachain, considered to be the mouth of the underworld. See CRUACHAN.

HENRY STREET Dublin, linking O'Connell Street with Mary Street; beside the General Post Office. The scene of bitter fighting after the GPO was abandoned in the Easter Rising, 1916, and where The O'Rahilly died. C.P. 355.

HIBERNIAN ACADEMY Royal Hibernian Academy now at 25 Ely Place, Dublin; once the home of Oliver St John Gogarty, friend of Yeats. A. 82.

HILL OF ALLEN, see ALMHUIN. Ex. 14, 15, 28.

HILL SEAT OF LAIGHEN Dun Ailinne or Ailenn, now Knock-haulin near Kilcullen, County Kildare, a hill fort. The oldest residence of the Kings of Leinster. Impressive megalithic remains. The hill fort alleged to be built by a prehistoric King Mes Delmonn. Like Almain called 'Almhuin' by Yeats, Dun Ailinne was one of the seats of the Kings of Leinster. C.P. 463.

HILLSIDE GATE Not traceable, though Yeats says it is in a village in Leinster. M. 15, 16, 17.

HOLY WELL Clogher Holy Well, County Sligo, of which St. Attracta was the Patron Saint. She received the veil from Saint Patrick and maintained a Hospital or House of Hospitality for travellers at Killaraght, County Sligo, near Holy Well. Also the area where the Costellos lived. It is from St. Attracta that Kiltartan derived its name. See KILTARTAN. M. 204.

HOSPITAL LANE At Island Bridge, Dublin, beside the Kilmainham Royal Hospital. M. 15, 16.

HOWTH CASTLE County Dublin, 9 mile N.E. of Dublin. Dating from 1564 when it was built by the St. Lawrence family who had been granted the district by Henry II. Remembered for the story of the abduction of the young heir from the bawn of the castle by Grace O'Malley, (Grainne Ni Mhaille), Queen of the Western Isles, who, being affronted on one unexpected occasion when she could not get in, took the heir in her galley back to County Mayo and did not return him until she got a promise that the castle would never be closed at meal time, and that an extra place would be set for an unexpected guest. To this day a spare place is set at the St. Lawrence table. A. 63.

HOWTH County Dublin. The word 'Howth' is derived from the Danish word 'Hovud', the older name being Beann Eadair; Eadar's Peak. Howth was a favourite hunting ground of Finn and his companions. The High King, Crimthann Nea Nair of the early 1st c., is buried on the Hill of Howth. The rocky islet of Ireland's Eye is off-shore. In 1880 the Yeats family moved from London to Howth where they lived until they moved to Rathgar in 1883. A. 32, 55, 60, 61, 76, 79. C.P. 348.

ILLETON Illerton, in the townland of Creganore parish of Kilchriest. Co. Galway. Locally written Elerton. Remains of a small oratory, and graveyard for unbaptised children. Holy well with cure for blindness, although the name of the saint is not known, but it may be a corruption of the Irish Word 'Ailithre', meaning turas or pilgrimage. M. 253.

INCHY County Galway. Derived from two islands in Coole lake. M. 61, 63, 65. Pl. 115.

INCHY WOOD Incha Wood. One of the Seven Woods of Coole, Co. Galway. It is the nearest wood to the one planted by Lady Gregory called by her 'The Isabella Wood', on the other side of it is a wood called the Fox Rock, but Yeats refers to it as Pairc na Carraig. M. 65, 68. C.P. 469. A. 378, 390.

INISFAIL the island of destiny, a poetic name for Ireland. E&I. 258.

INISHMAAN Inis Meain, the middle island, County Galway. Smaller than Inishmore, yet bigger than Inisheer, the east island; the third island to make up the Aran Islands. Dominated by Dun Conor an impressive stone fort. Rich in prehistoric sites and ruined churches.

Irish survives as the spoken language, though Liam O'Flaherty says that many of the inhabitants speak English with a cockney accent, being descendants of soldiers from Cromwell's army. A. 343.

INISHMORE Arainn Mhor, the big island, County Galway. According to legend the Firbolg found refuge here after the Battle of Moytirra and built the Dun Aengus, the most impressive building of its type in Europe; on the edge of 300 foot cliff, it symbolises the last stand of a desperate race. It contains three concentric ramparts interlaced with an additional screen of defence and its chevaux-de-frise of pointed stones.

In Christian times it became one of the most celebrated monastic sites, with St. Enda its greatest saint. Many internationally famous scholars studied here. The island is dotted with pre-Christian and Christian remains. Garrisoned by Cromwellians.

Synge came here on the advice of Yeats (1896) to study native vernacular and traditional lore, which inspired *Riders to the Sea*. Robert O'Flaherty filmed *Man of Aran* here with a local cast in 1934. Irish is spoken. A. 343.

INISHMURRAY Inis Muireadhaigh off the County Sligo coast four miles from Streedagh Point, called after St. Muireadhach, Bishop of Killala. Monastery founded in 6th c. by St. Molaise; still in such a good state of preservation as to indicate the layout of early monastic settlements. Because of its isolation, preservation is unusually good. Interesting features are separate churches and even cemeteries for men and women; renowned for its "cursing stones". The Island was one of the first places in Ireland to be ravaged by the Vikings.

The dwindling population of less than fifty was removed to the mainland in 1947. C.P. 25.

INNISFREE Inisfree, Inisfraoich. The heathery island, a small island in Lough Gill, County Sligo, just off-shore from Killery Mountain. The inspiration of Yeats's most popular poem. A. 72, 153. CP. 44.

INSULA TRINITATIS Trinity Island on Lough Key, County Roscommon, where Clarus Mac Maillin founded a monastery for the Praemonstratention Order (1215). *The Annals of Lough Ce* were compiled on it. Holds the graves of the ill-starred lovers, Una Bhan and Thomas Laidir Mac Costello. The monastery was one of the most important in Connacht in mediaeval Ireland. Una and Costello were not buried as Yeats wrote inside the Abbey of Insula Trinitatis, but outside the walls. In time, two trees grew up from the graves and intertwined in a lover's knot. M. 208, 209, 210.

INVER AMERGIN The mouth of the Avoca River, County

Wicklow, where Amergin the Druid landed with the Milesians. He is alleged to have compiled the history of the earlier inhabitants of the country and to have written the first poem in Ireland. He was one of the sons of Milesius by his second wife Scota, daughter of a Pharaoh (Nectonebis). One of the earliest names for Ireland was Scota. C.P. 17.

ITH Magh Itha. The Lagan Valley, County Donegal, called after Ith, one of the Milesian settlers. Near the mouth of the river Finn, where it enters Lough Foyle. St. Patrick built a Church there. C.P. 17.

KERRY Ciarraighe, The Lady Ceasair, leader of the first invaders landed at Dunmore, County Kerry, and according to one claim is buried there. The Milesians landed in Kerry, and Amergin the Druid sang the first poem composed in Ireland. On their way to Tara they met Eiriu, Fodhla and Banba, three goddesses who gave their names to the country. Scota, wife of Milesius, slain in battle, was buried here.

The mother goddess of Munster, Anu, or Danu, the goddess of prosperity, ancestress of the Tuatha de Danann, gave her name to a mountain in Kerry called The Paps of Anu (or The Two Paps) Da Chich Anann.

The Caillech Beare, or Hag of Beare, the foster mother of the ancestor of a Kerry tribe, is a popular figure in Irish folklore with monuments in many parts of the country called after her as far from Kerry as Antrim. The lament for the Old Woman of Beare, links Beare Island with Sliabh-na-mban-Femen (caller 'Knockfefin' by Yeats).

Fintann, patron of poets of the race of Lady Ceasair is alleged to have returned from his haunts in Kerry to relate the history of Ireland to St. Patrick. His grave is on Lough Derg on the Shannon. A. 217. C.P. 354. E. & I. 324, 327, 334, 340. Pl. 439.

KILBECANTY Cill Becnata, County Galway the church of Becnata or Beacanta (Pronounced 'Kilbecnty'.) M. 26.

KILCHRIEST Cill Chriost, Christ's Church, County Galway. A most unusual name in Ireland where churches are usually called after saints; a parish between Essertkelly and Loughrea. M. 214, 215.

KILCOLMAN CASTLE Two and a half miles N.E. of Buttevant at the Mallow-Charleville road, County Cork: originally a stronghold of the Earl of Desmond, forfeited after the suppression of the Desmond Rebellion (1598) and given to Edmund Spenser. It was here he wrote part of *The Fairie Queen*. The castle was burned (1598); Spenser's son thought to have perished in the fire and Edmund Spenser returned to England. E. & I. 360, 361.

KILCLUAN Cill-Cluain, now Kilcloony the church of the meadow near Ballinasloe, County Galway. Site of 7th c. church of St Grellan, patron saint of the district, and site of a bardic school of poetry of the O'Higgini family, hereditary poets of County Sligo. Pl. 304.

KILDARE Cill Dara, County in Leinster: contains the mythological sites of Allmhuin and Dun Ailenn; the principal foundation of St. Bridget (Mary of the Gael); the Japanese Gardens at the National Stud at Tully; The Curragh Camp, The Curragh race-course and stables, Mary Yeats, née Butler, inherited lands in Co. Kildare, which were sold by John Butler Yeats, the poet's father.

KILDARE STREET Dublin, between St. Stephens Green and Nassau Street; contains the Oireachtas (House of Parliament), the National Museum, National Library, Metropolitan School of Art and the Kildare Street Club. A. 79, 476.

KILDARE STREET LIBRARY See NATIONAL LIBRARY.

KILDARE STREET MUSEUM See NATIONAL MUSEUM.

KILGLASS Cill Molaise, in an old M.S. called Kilmolasse, County Sligo. There were three castles in this parish belonging to the Mac Firbisi, the hereditary Ollaves to the O'Dowda, Kings of North Connacht, who kept a hereditary school of law at

Lecan sometimes called Lecan Mac Firbisi. Here they compiled two of the greatest sources of Irish records, *The Book of Lecan* and *The Yellow Book of Lecan*. The tomb of the Mac Firbisi is in the graveyard of Kilglass Church. Pl. 81.

KILKENNY Cill Channaigh, the capital of County Kilkenny. A most interesting town with its Georgian architecture, dominated by the castle. Incorporated as a town in 1204 by William Marshall son-in-law of Strongbow. In time it became the principal seat of the great Anglo-Irish Butler family who became in turn Earls, Marquesses and Dukes of Ormonde from whom Yeats was descended.

Parliaments were held in Kilkenny in the 13th, 14th and 15th centuries. In 1366 the famous Statute of Kilkenny was passed which forbade English settlers from using the Irish language, adopting Irish names, wearing Irish apparel or intermarriage with the Irish people. It did not prevail. In 1642 Kilkenny was the seat of Catholic Confederate Parliament.

Swift, Congreve, Farquhar and Berkeley went to school in Kilkenny. Ex. 91, 333.

KILLALA Cill Alaidh on Killala Bay near Ballina, County Mayo. St. Muirreadach patron saint of a church founded by St. Patrick. Round Tower. Scene of the French forces landing in support of the 1798 Rebellion.

Fine ruins of Moyne Abbey, a 15th c. Franciscan Friary, and Rathfran Abbey, a 13th c. Dominican Friary in the vicinity. Rosserk Abbey (See BALLINA) is between Killala and Ballina.

Neighbourhood is rich in megalithic monuments. Pl. 75, 87. A. 421.

KILLALOE Cill Dalua, Dalua's Church, County Clare. A small town in a beautiful setting on the banks of the Shannon. Brian Boru made it the capital of Munster in 12th c. Before that time it had been an important ecclesiastical site and became the see of the diocese of Killaloe. Retains well preserved ecclesiastical ruins of considerable interest. Brian Boru's palace of Kincora was in and about the site of the present

Catholic Church. The adjacent oratory is that of St. DaLua, removed and rebuilt in 1929 from Friar's Island when the island was submerged during the construction of the Shannon hydroelectric works. An old cross-shaft has an inscription on it in Runes and Ogham. See Kincora. Ex. 185.

KILLEENAN Cillinin, St. Finans Church, County Galway, about three miles from Craughwell. Blind Raftery, the Gaelic poet from County Mayo, (1784–1834), who sang the beauty of Mary Hynes of Ballylee, is buried here. His grave was unmarked until Lady Gregory erected a headstone on it. Ex. 202, 203.

KILMACOWEN Cill Mac Owen, County Sligo. The church of Owen's son. Townland of that name, but no barony as mentioned in *The Land of Hearts Desire*. A Holy Well named after St. Patrick and a stone with the imprint of the saints' knees on it between Ballysadare and Knocknarea. Pl. 53.

KILRONAN Cill Ronain, Ronan's Church, Inishmore (Aran Island) County Galway. Name is derived from Saint Ronan's monastery. The biggest village on the island, with a pier at which the steamer from Galway lands passengers. Nearby a holy well, Toberonan. E. & I. 330.

KILTARTAN CROSS. M. 24. C.P. 152.

KILTARTAN RIVER County Galway, rises in Sliabh Echgthe or Slieve Aughty and may join underground the Ballylee River. The river disappears underground through a swallow-hole named Poli Tufhail (Poul Touchall) in the townland of Castletown which gets its name from Ballinamantane Castle, sometimes incorrectly called Kiltartan Castle. It surfaces beside a monument to Sir W. Gregory behind Kiltartan Catholic Church, flows overground for half a mile on the way then underground again until it surfaces in Raheen, and thence to Coole Lake from which it finally goes underground until it enters the sea at Kinvara. Pl. 462.

KILVARNET Cill Bhearnais, the church in the gap. A townland near the village of Ballinacarrow, County Sligo, with the remains of an old church. The present parish of Collooney was originally known as the parish of Ballysodare and Kilvarnet about which Dr O.Rourke wrote *The History of Ballysodare and Kilvarnet.* C.P. 82.

KINADIFE Kyle-na-Dyfa, Coill na Daibhche, the wood of the cauldron (i.e. hollow shape) in Slieve Echgthe between Illerton and Scalp, County Galway. M. 253.

KINCORA Ceann Coradh, the head of the weir, on the river Shannon, Killaloe, County Clare. Kincora is inseparable from Brian Boru, chief of the Dal Cais, who became the greatest High King of Ireland, in fact as well as name. He ended the Viking invasion at the battle of Clontarf on Good Friday, 1014, but was killed by Broder the Dane in the moment of his triumph. Brian's reign and the Glories of Kincora are enshrined in Mac Liagh's "War of the Gael and the Gall."

Kincora cannot boast the antiquity of Tara, Emain Macha or Cruachan, but it had its moment of glory when Brian moved the capital of Munster to Kincora. Its strategic significance overlooking a ford on the Shannon is obvious. A. 483, 491, 505.

KING'S COUNTY The Plantation of Laoise and Ui Failghe in the reign of Mary I who created the names Queen's County and King's County in honour of herself and her husband King Philip II of Spain. Since the Treaty (1922) they have reverted to their old names of Leix and Offaly. The inhabitants of Leix, descended from Conal Cernach of The Red Branch Knights, known as Loigis. The Pass of the Plumes was the scene of a great victory by Rory O'More over the English forces under Essex (1599).

The Rock of Dunamase with its imposing ruins of a castle was the scene of war from the time of the Vikings to Cromwell. Given by Dermot Mac Morrow to Strongbow in 14th c., owned by the Mortimers, heirs to the throne of England. Stronghold of the O'Mores of Ui Faighle, greatest of the perpetual despoilers of The Pale, and owners of *"The Book of Leinster."*

Durrow, from which the famous Irish M.S. *"The Book of Durrow"* takes its name, is in this County. A. 20. M. 43.

The original Abbey Theatre, Lower Abbey Street, Dublin, which was burned down in 1951

Thoor Ballylee, near Gort, Co. Galway.

Above: Coole Park, Gort, Co. Galway. *Below*: Lissadell, Co. Sligo.

The Autograph Tree at Coole (a copper beech).

Glencar Waterfall, Co. Leitrim.

Castle Island, Lough Kay.

Lough Gill, Co. Sligo.

Above: Poulnabrone Dolmen, the Burren, Co. Clare. *Below*: Gallerus Oratory, Co. Kerry.

Above: St. Patrick's Rock, the Rock of Cashel, Co. Tipperary. *Below*: Corcomroe Abbey, Abbeywest Townland, Co. Clare.

Above: Crianan Ailich Fort, Carrowreach Townland, Co. Donegal. *Below*: Dun Aengus, Innishmore, Aran Islands.

Above: The Catstone on Usnach Hill, Co. Westmeath, "the Centre of Ireland".
Below: Megalithic Tomb, Moytirra East, Co. Sligo.

Knocknarea, Co. Sligo, with Lough Gill in the foreground.

O'Rorke's Castle on the River Bonnet, between Dromahaire and Lough Gill. Dervorgilla eloped from here with Dermot MacMorrough.

The Hawk's Rock, close to the Hawk's Well, Tullaghan, Coolaney, Co. Sligo.

Drumcliff Cross, Co. Sligo.

Ben Bulben from Drumcliff Churchyard, Co. Sligo, with W. B. Yeats's grave in the foreground.

KING CONCHUBAR'S COUNTRY See ULADH. Pl. 171.

KINGSTOWN Dun Laoghaire, Laoghaire's Fort, County Dublin. The name was changed to Kingstown in 1821 to commemorate the visit to Ireland of George IV. The original name was restored after Independence. James Joyce lived at 23 Carysfort Avenue (1892–1902) and later at the Martello Tower at the "Forty Foot" when it was owned by Oliver Gogarty. The tower figures in *Ulysses*. Lord Edward FitzGerald lived at 'Frescati' beside Merrion Avenue. Ex. 188.

KINSALE Cionn Tsaile the head of the sea, County Cork. A Georgian seaport of great charm. The defeat of the Irish and Spanish forces at Kinsale in 1601 by the English, sealed the doom of the Gaelic civilization, followed by The Flight of the Earls. James II landed here (1689) in an attempt to regain his English throne, and sailed from here to exile after his fainthearted fight at the battle of the Boyne (1690).

The *Lusitania* was torpedoed and sunk by a German submarine in 1915 off The Old Head of Kinsale, Sir Hugh Lane, nephew of Lady Gregory being one of the 1,000 drowned, almost within sight of his birthplace.

Kinsale was always a stronghold of the Protestant English colony. Until the end of the 18th c. neither Catholics nor Irish were allowed to live within its walls. Had an English garrison until 1922. A. 493. M. 15. C.P. 26.

KINVARA Ceann-Mhara, the head of the sea. A market town at the tip of Kinvara Bay, County Galway. Nearby is 16th c. Dunguaire Castle (Dungory) formerly owned by the Martyns of Tullira, built on the site of the palace of Guaire the Hospitable, King of Connacht. Both Guaire and his castle figure in numerous folk tales, notably the flight of the dishes from Guaire's table to the cell of his kinsman St. Colman in Oughtmama by the route still known as Bothar na Mias, The Way of the Dishes. A few miles south is Daras House. (See DURAS) M. 27, 45, 225. Pl. 116, 117, 121, 332, 344.

KNOCKFEFIN Sliabh-na-mBan, Femhinn, the mountain of the

women of Feimhenn (Femen). Now known as Slievenamon, County Tipperary, a fairy palace named Sid ar Femun, home of Bodb-Derg son of Dagda in which the sidh enchanted Finn Mac Cool. The mountain took its name from the women of this palace. Te and Men, the wives of two Bards of the Tuatha de Danann. Referred to in *The Pursuit of Giolla Dacker and his Horse.*

Oengus Mac Og of Brugh-na-Boinne found Caer, with her maidens in the shape of swans on Loch Bel Drecon in Magh Femen, the plain of Femen. C.P. 444.

KNOCKNAGUR Cnoc-na-fCorr. The hill of the clucking hens. Not a townland but a local name for part of the townland of Kilcreevanty near Tuam, County Galway. Cathal More of the Wine Red Hand, King of Connacht, founded a nunnery here (1200). M. 9.

KNOCKNAREA County Sligo. Cnoc naRiaghadh, Cnoc no riogh. Authorities give different interpretations of the meaning; the hill of the king and the hill of the executions. The former is more likely because Miscaun Maeve on the summit of Knocknarea was the burial place of Eoghan Bel, the last pagan King of Connacht who fell in the battle of Sligo, until his corpse was stolen by his enemies from the north and re-buried face downwards near the present town of Sligo.

Popular tradition holds that Queen Maeve is buried there, but this is improbable. She was killed in old age by a stone from a catapult on Inis Clothrann in Lough Ree much nearer the royal burial ground of Reilig na Riogh at Cruachan. Therefore more likely than Knocknarea, with which she had no association, nor, indeed with County Sligo at all.

MSS testify that "Maeve was buried at Cruachan which was the proper burial ground of her race, her body having been removed by her people from Dun Medhbha, for they deemed it more honourable to have her interred at Cruachan". F. J. Byrne, *The High Kings of Ireland*, writes

"The saga says that Eoghan Bel was buried upright at Raith Ua Fiachrach on Knocknarea, facing northward with his red spear still in his hand. As long as he remained thus the Northerns

could never defeat Connacht. Eventually the Ui Neill took coun-
sel and disinterred his body, burying it face downwards at
Oenagh Locha Gile, the Assembly Place of Lough Gill, Irish
Kings and High Kings." A. 78, 262, 268, 284. M. 57, 88, 90,
93, 150, 237. C.P. 24, 61, 409. Pl. 17, 641.

KNOCKNASHEE Cnoc na Sidhe, hill of the fairy palace. A
round hill near Achonry, County Sligo. The townland has the
same meaning as the hill, alleged to be the headquarters of the
sidhe of N. Connacht. C.P. 24.

KYLE-DORTHA Coill-Dorracha, the dark wood at Coole,
County Galway, destroyed by burning; one of the Seven Woods
of Coole. C.P. 469.

KYLE-na-NO Coill-na-gno, the nut or hazel wood; one of the
Seven Woods of Coole, County Galway. C.P. 143, 175, 469.

LABAN A small village near Ardrahan, County Galway. Stained
glass windows commissioned for the church by Edward Martyn
of Tullira. The imposing entrance gates and pillars came from
Roxborough on the break up of the estate. A. 402. Pl. 465.

LAIGHEN Coicid Laigin, the fifth or province of Leinster. A
tribal name derived from spears called laigin used for the first
time in Ireland, in the 3rd c. Leinster was ruled from the hill
fort of Dun Ailenn, built by King Mes Delmonn. The legend of
the origin of Leinster told in the saga, *The Destruction of Dinn
Rig.* The tribe formed a contingent of Maeve's army in *The
Tain,* of which she was jealous so she divided them up among
the other troops of her army when her husband Ailill, a Laigin,
refused to have them destroyed. Two of the royal seats of Leinster were Dun Ailenn and Almain.

Literature and art in the province are represented by *The
Book of Kells* 8th c. *The Book of Durrow* and *The Book of
Leinster.* C.P. 463. E. & I. 397.

LAMBAY ISLAND Rachra, Rechru, Reachra. Lambay is of
Danish origin, Lamb-ey, Lamb's Island, County Dublin. St.

Columcille founded a monastery on it. Ravaged by Vikings. A. 59.

LEAP CASTLE County Offaly, Leim-Ui-Bhanain, "O'Bannon's leap" (F.M.) The Haunted mansion burned down in 1922 was on the site of a castle of the O'Carrolls of Ely, an Irish Family noted for its patronage of the arts in mediaeval Ireland. Two School Invitations of Margaret O'Carroll in the late 15th c. are recorded in detail in many Irish Annals and more recently in a poem by Aubery de Vere. V. 224.

LEINSTER ROAD In Rathmines, Dublin. A. 94.

LEITRIM – Liatroim. Grey Ridge. The County of Leitrim takes its name from village of same name. It was the end of the tragic march of O'Sullivan Beare from Bantry, County Cork to sanctuary with O'Rorke of Breiffny in 17th c. E&I. 246.

LETTERKENNY Leitir Ceanainn, the hillside of the O'Canannains, County Donegal. It was the stronghold of the O'Canannains, Kings of Tir Connell before being ousted by the O'Donnells. The inauguration place of the O'Canannains is nearby. It is now the cathedral town of the diocese of Raphoe. The last battle in Ulster in the 17th c. Parliamentarian War took place a few miles away when the Catholic forces led by the Bishop of Clogher were annihilated. Ex. 74.

LIBERTIES Originally referred to different districts in Dublin, until finally the term became identified with an area bounded by Dublin castle, the Quays, Blackpitts and St James Gate. Jonathan Swift, Dean of St. Patrick's was born at Hoey's Court. He became known as "Monarch of the Liberties and King of the Mob." 'The Brazen Head' inn in Bridge Street was frequented by Grattan, O'Connell, Burke, Emmet and Tone. The Tailors' Hall in Back Lane, once the headquarters of the Tailors' Guild, restored by the Irish Georgian Society, 1972.

A Huguenot colony settled in the Liberties in 1685, heralding an era of industrialisation for the Liberties.

Marsh's Library in Saint Patrick's Close is the oldest public library in Ireland. Founded 1702.

Many of the names of places in the Liberties are changed and are remembered only in the ballads of blind Zosimus. M. 47.

LIMERICK Luimneach, a city at the mouth of the Shannon, means the mouth of the river. City established by Vikings at Inis Sibtonn, one of their most important strategic centres for raids along the coast and inland via the Shannon to Lough Ree, until Brian Boru drove them out. Henceforth was the centre of power of the O'Briens. King John erected a fortified castle (still standing) and a bridge. Edward Bruce made it his headquarters for a time. Beseiged by Cromwell. In the William-ite War, Limerick bravely defended by Sarsfield against over-whelming odds; the Flight of the Wild Geese (under Sarsfield) after the breaking of the Treaty alleged to have been signed on the Treaty Stone beside Thomond Bridge (1691). Has fine Georgian streets, many being allowed to decay sadly. A. 35. M. 236. Pl. 96. B. 11. Ex. 75, 411.

LIFFEY Rises in the Wicklow Mountains and flows into Dublin Bay. City of Dublin originated near the ford of the hurdles on the ancient road from Tara to Garman (Wexford). A. 94. B. 11.

LISSADELL Lis-a-Doill, the fort of the blind man, County Sligo. Once owned by a branch of the family of O'Dalaigh, hereditary poets free of tribute (or rent) by virtue of their profession.

In the early part of the 18th c. the Gore family came into possession of Lissadell. The present neo-classical house was built of Ballysadare limestone, 1832–4. C.P. 263.

LOCHLANN, a mythical country inhabited by the Fomorians. It appears in the myths concerning Lugh and the sons of Tuireann. One of their penances for having killed Lugh's father was to give three shouts on the Hill of Miochaoin in the north of Loch-lann. VP. 749.

LOUGH DERG A small desolate lake on the borders of County Donegal and County Fermanagh. Known since Middle Ages as St. Patrick's Purgatory, as St. Patrick was alleged to have fasted there and had a vision of the next world. Became so well known for its pilgrimage that many visited it until the pligrimage was banned because of excesses (1497). Nonetheless it continued and still is the most important pilgrimage in Ireland; takes place between 1st June and the 15th August and lasts for three days, fasting with one night's vigil. An English monk wrote *Purgatorium Patricii* (1190) which describes a vision seen there (1153) by an English knight. C.P. 360. Ex. 266, 267. E. & I. 185.

LOUGH GILL Loch Gile, the bright lake, County Sligo. One of the most romantically beautiful lakes in Ireland, immortalised by Yeats, in his best known poem 'The Lake Isle of Innisfree.' Overlooked by Knocknarea, Ben Bulben, Slieve Daeane, Slish Wood, Dooney Rock, O'Rorke's Table. Its islands include Inisfree, Church Island (Inis Mor), Gallagher's Island and many smaller ones. The best panoramic view of it is from The Green Road about half mile beyond Markievicz Park. A circular tour of the lake passes many of the places mentioned by the poet. A. 71, 153. M. 101, 171.

LOUGH GREINE Loch Graney, County Clare, fed by the river Graney which rises in Loch Attorick in Slieve Echgthe, possibly gets its name from Grainne, daughter of Finn Mac Cool. According to O'Dugan's important Topographical Poem it is named after the district of Grain. Celebrated in the poem "cuairt an Mhean-Oiche" (*The Midnight Court*) by Bryan Merryman, a native of the district, translated by Frank O'Connor and others. M. 25, 216, 222.

LOUGH IA Loch Da Ghe, The lake of the two geese, high up on Sliabh da Ean, now Slieve Daeane (Bird Mountain) in County Sligo. Name derived from the story of two birds drowned in the Lake. M. 79.

LOUGH KAY, LOUGH CAY, Lough Cé, Lough Key, near Boyle, County Roscommon. Best over-all view is from the Rock of Doon on the Boyle–Ballyfarnon road. The MacDermots, Princes of Moylurg, ruled that territory from Carraigh Mhic

Diarmada until the Williamite War. The Praemonstratentian Abbey on Trinity Island owned extensive possessions as far as Gallagher's Island on Lough Gill and in parts of Mayo and Galway. *The Annals of Loch Cé* were compiled there. A. 253. M. 208. See CASTLE ROCK.

LOUGH LEATH, LOCH LIATH, in Sliabh Fuad (now the Fews) County Armagh. It was at Loch Liath that Cuchulain got his two war horses, Liath Macha and Saiglin.

The capture of Liath Macha is described in *The Feast of Bricriu.*

Liath Macha returned to the enchanted lake after the death of Cuchulain. M. 79. VP. 802. (Pl. 669, 699.)

LOUGHREA Baile Locha Riabhach. The town of the grey lake, County Galway. Crannogs (lake dwellings), ring forts and the famous Turoe Stone 1st c. phallic stone with La Tène sculpture. Ruins of Carmelite friary.

Findabhair, Queen of Connacht, who lived at Cnoc Findabhrach, died of shame because a poet wrote in her praise and she had no gold to give him.

St Brendan's Cathedral is well known for its stained glass windows by Evie Hone, Sarah Purser and other Dublin school artists. A. 392. M. 214.

LOUGH SWILLY Loch Suile, or Suilech (Four Masters) County Donegal. Gets its name from river Swilly (the river of the whirlpools) which flows into Lough Swilly. Associated with the treacherous kidnapping of the fifteen year old Red Hugh O'Donnell, (1587) and his incarceration in the Bermingham Tower of Dublin Castle until his escape to the Wicklow Hills (1591). This incident was one of the causes of the Nine Year War which ended in disaster at Kinsale (1601) and the end of Gaelic civilization in Ireland. It was followed by The Flight of the Earls from Rathmullan on the shores of Lough Swilly (1607), and then by the disastrous Plantation of Ulster, the results of which continue to this day. Wolfe Tone landed from the French battleship 'La Hoche' with three hundred French-

men on board at Rathmullen on Lough Swilly (1798) E. & I.
362.

LUGNAGALL Lug Na nGall, the hollow of the strangers, not as
Yeats defines it "the Steep Place of the Strangers" (M. 183). In
County Sligo. "Lug" means hollow. Is a townland in Glencar
valley at the foot of Cope's Mountain. M. 183, 242, 243, 245,
248. C.P. 50.

MACROOM Ma Chromtha, the sloping field, County Cork. Seat
of the MacCarthy family. Cromwell gave the estate to Admiral
Penn, father of the founder of Pennsylvania, who lost it at the
Restoration. Also the seat of a branch of the MacSwineys of
Scotland, (gallowglasses or professional soldiers.)
   Nearby, Art O'Leary was killed. The latter is of "Caoine Art
O'Laoghaire" by his wife, Eileen Dubh O'Connell, a most beau-
tiful Irish lament, (translated by Frank O'Connor, *Kings, Lords
and Commons*). Thomas Davis (1815–1845) co-founder of 'The
Nation' and one of the guiding spirits of the Young Ireland
Movement was born here. A. 411. Ex. 74.

MAGH AI Machaire Connacht, the great plain in County Roscommon dominated by Cruachan. It extended from Elphin to
Roscommon town, and from Castlerea to Strokestown. The
ancestral lands of the O'Conors, Kings of Connacht. C.P. 453.

MANOR HAMILTON Cluainin Ui Ruairc, O'Rorke's little
meadow; originally in Breiffny (O'Rorke territory), now in
County Leitrim. Named after Sir Frederick Hamilton who was
given lands there by Charles I. Associated with the sacking of
Sligo Abbey (1641). M. 178.

MANSION HOUSE Dawson Street, Dublin. Official residence of
Lord Mayors since 1715. The Declaration of Independence and
the Treaty of 1921 signed in the Round Room. Yeats was right
in declaring that this fine Queen Anne (1705) building had
been ruined by Victoriana such as stucco, a large cast iron
porch and plate glass. A. 203, 227, 366. B. 9, 10. Ex. 409.

MARKET STREET, SLIGO Leading off Castle Street. Present day Dominican friary, beside site of original 12th c. castle of Sligo built by Maurice Fitzgerald. M. 71.

MARKREE Collooney, County Sligo, Markree Castle built by a descendant of Cornet Cooper of Cromwell's army, who married Maire Rua O'Brien to enable her to retain the family property in County Clare for her son. Early 19th century entrance gates, walls and lodges are a splendid example of Picturesque gothic. See Kenneth Clark, *The Gothic Revival*. Well known observatory. Ex. 347n.

MAYNOOTH Ma Nuad, Nua's Plain, County Kildare. St. Patrick's College the most famous seminary in the British Isles, now a college of the National University. Large collection of valuable MSS. Ruins of Geraldine castle of the Fitzgeralds. B. 27.

MAYO Muigheo, County Mayo derives its name from a small village of that name – the plain of the yew trees – where St. Colman founded a monastery in 7th c. referred to in the *Annals* as Magheo-na-Saxon because many English monks followed St. Colman there after he left his See of Lindisfarne. A. 96, 443. C.P. 149. M. 19, 41, 42, 55, 98, 199, 201, 229. Pl. 465, 667. Ex. 98.

MEATH Mide, middle, Coicid Mide, one of the five provinces of Ireland. Since the creation of counties known as County Meath. Originally it included Longford, Offaly and Westmeath. In the old Irish period the kingdom of Brega included the present County Meath with parts of the Counties Louth and Dublin.

Tara was the capital until it was cursed by St Ruadan in 6th c. after which Dun na Sciath at Lough Ennell in County Westmeath superseded Tara. Pl. 37, 673, 674. A. 21.

MECHANICS' INSTITUTE THEATRE See ABBEY THEATRE. Ex. 124.

MEMORY HARBOUR Rosses Point, County Sligo. The name of one of the best-known of Jack Yeats' watercolours (1900).

Subject : the village of Rosses Point from the mainland with the Metal Man in the middle of the harbour; in the foreground a man walking, in the distance, the sea, sky and sailing boat. A fine, carefully drawn watercolour, owned by the poet. A. 52.

MERVILLE Sligo. Once the home of Yeats' Pollexfen grandparents where he stayed; now 'The Nazareth Home' for old people and orphans. The entrance is from Church Hill, on the road from the cathedrals to Macherabuie (Maugheraboy). A. 18, 51.

METAL BRIDGE Dublin, facing Crampton Quay. Also known as the Halfpenny Bridge from the days when a tax of a halfpenny was paid to cross the Liffey on foot. A single-arch, cast-iron footbridge, built in 1816, originally known as Wellington Bridge. A. 94.

METROPOLITAN SCHOOL OF ART, See ARTS SCHOLS. Ex. 193.

MIDHIR'S HILL Slieve Golry near Ardagh, County Longford. Bri Leith or Sid Midhir was one of the most famous otherworld dwellings in Ireland. Oengus was at fosterage with Midhir at Bri Leith. This is the setting of *The Wooing of Etain*, the goddess of sovereignty, as told in *The Book of the Dun Cow*. One of the prerogatives of the King of Tara was "The bilberries of Bri Leith". C.P. 471.

MOCHARABUIEE Machaire Buí, the yellow plain, on the S.W. outskirts of Sligo leading to Carrowmore, Cloverhill and the Glen Road round Knocknarea. This townland is and has always been known as Magheraboy. C.P. 82.

MOLESWORTH HALL Dublin. *The Hour Glass* by Yeats, *Twenty Five* by Lady Gregory (1903), and *The Shadowy Waters* (1904), received their first productions by the Irish National Theatre Society here. After a performance in this Hall, Yeats appealed from the stage for financial help to aid the Society and Miss Horniman, English theatre manager and patron said, "I will give you a theatre." Ex. 102, 181.

MOONEEN Moneen, Móinín, the little bog, adjoining Esserkelly, near Ardrahan, County Galway. Fort. Mary Hynes was found dead in Mooneen. C.P. 150.

MOUGHOROW Maugherow Magh Eabha or Machaire Eabha, a level plain lying between Benbulben and the sea, County Sligo. Not a townland, but a half-parish. The Gore-Booth sisters knew it and its inhabitants intimately, and Eva set many of her poems in this area of which the best known is "The Little Waves of Breiffny". M. 96.

MOYTURA, MOYTIRRA, from Magh Tuiridh, the plain of the pillars, or Magh Turach the towered plain, overlooking Lough Arrow, County Sligo. Site of battle in which the Tuatha de Danann finally overthrew the Firbolgs. The Danann forces landed in a mist on Slieve Anieran in Breiffny : Goban, the smith, made the weapons of war on this mountain for the Danann.

Eochaid MacEirc, the Firbolg, overcome by thirst, left the battle field for a drink. The Danann hid all the streams and rivers so he travelled as far as the strand called Traigh Eothail (Beltra) near Ballisadare. There he was attacked by the Danann, and all were killed. Great cairns were erected over their graves on the strand which became one of the wonders of Ireland because the tidal waters never covered it. Pl. 49. VP. 810, 813.

MUCKANISH Inis-na- Muc, County Clare promontory of the seals (often called sea-pigs on West Coast) not far from Corcomroe, County Clare. Ruins of two castles of the O'Loghlins, Lords of Burren. Known as Mucanish Castle and Sean Mucanish Castle. (Muckanish is pronounced today as in Gaelic 'Mucnish'.)

St. Camain of Inis Cealtra, Regulus of Muc-Inish travelled to Eas Dara (Ballisodare) to meet St. Columcille at The Meeting of the Saints. Pl. 435.

MUIRTHEMNE plain in County Louth from the Cooley Mountains to the river Boyne. Called after Muirthemne, son of Breogan, whose sons gave their names to so many districts in

Ireland. Breogan, the father of Ith, was one of the leaders of the Milesians. Kian of the Danaan changed into the shape of a pig and joined a herd of swine to avoid capture by the Sons of Tuirenn. Is the site of the central fight in *The Tain*. C.P. 459, 463. Pl. 695. Ex. 3–13, 19, 29, 92, 371. E. & I. 335.

MULLINGAR Muileann Cearr, wry mill, County Westmeath. Several lakes in vicinity enshrined in folklore and history : Lough Derryvaragh (*The Children of Lir*); Lough Owel (where Malachy drowned Turgesius the Dane) and Lough Ennel, the seat of the Ui Neill (after the destruction of Tara) at Dun na Sciath on the lakeshore and the island stronghold of Cro-Inis. The Ulster forces camped hereabouts during *The Tain*. M. 90.

MUNICIPAL GALLERY OF MODERN ART Dublin Municipal Gallery and Municipal Gallery, formerly Charlemont House, Parnell Square, Dublin. The building is an 18th c. three-storeyed mansion (1762–5) built for the Earl of Charlemont, the 'Volunteer Earl' and great patron of the arts. The oval staircase and the drawing room are the only surviving interior features. In 1930 it was converted, when it became the Municipal Gallery of Modern Art. It contains many fine paintings including half the Hugh Lane collection (the other half is in London), and many portraits of friends of Yeats described in 'The Municipal Gallery Revisited'. A. 243, 397, 425. E. & I. 343. C.P. 368.

MUNSTER Coicid Mumu, the province of Munster. Now Mumhan. Sometimes referred to in old MSS as two fifths, that of Thomond and Desmond, roughly as Turlough O'Conor was to divide Munster in the 12th c. An older name for Munster was Iarmumu. In mythology there are three mother goddesses in Munster, Aibhill of Craig Liath, Anu mother of the gods in Kerry and Aine of Knockaney, County Limerick, the sun goddess. After the defeat of the Tuatha de Danann by the Milesians, their King retired to Munster. The Cailleach Berri originated in Kerry. Mumu is a geographical name of unknown origin, but Ulaid, Laigin and Connacht are tribal names. M. 213, 234. C.P. 51. A. 534. Pl. 663. Ex. 91.

NATIONAL GALLERY Dublin National Gallery. On the west side of Merrion Square, flanking the lawn of Leinster House. Opened 1864. Big collection of important paintings from all European schools of paintings. Includes an Irish section and the National Portrait Gallery. A. 81, 292.

NATIONAL LIBRARY Kildare Street, Dublin. Flanking the courtyard of Leinster House. Founded 1877, moved to its present Renaissance-type building in 1890. Over half a million volumes, and a large Department of Manuscripts. Yeats refers to it as the Kildare Street Library. A. 69, 91. Ex. 111.

THE NATIONAL MUSEUM and Dublin Museum, Kildare Street, Dublin 1884. Opposite the National Library, flanking Leinster House. Valuable collections of archaeological and botanical objects. Irish treasures from early historic times such as the Ardagh Chalice (8th c.), the 'Tara' Brooch (8th c.), the Moylough Belt Reliquary (8th c.), and the Cross of Cong (12th c.). Hugh Lane, Lady Gregory's nephew and art connoisseur, once applied for the curatorship but was passed over in favour of Papal Count George Plunkett, an apparently less qualified candidate, thus causing Yeats to write 'An Appointment' (1909), one of his first satirical poems. A. 90. V. 45.

THE NATIONAL UNIVERSITY Founded 1852, opened two years later with Dr John Henry Newman as Rector at Clanwilliam House, St Stephen's Green, Dublin, where it was in Yeats' time. In 1909 became a College of the National University of Ireland. Today more than 8,000 full-time students, now in new buildings on 300 acres in Donnybrook, a residential suburb of Dublin, and 1,300 acres for the Faculty of Agriculture at Celbridge, as well as Newman House, Dublin. A. 202, 208. B. 10. Ex. 264, 409.

O'CONNELL BRIDGE Over the Liffey, Dublin, at the S. end of O'Connell Street; named after the Liberator. A reconstruction (1880) of Gandon's Carlisle Bridge (1792). A. 94. E. & I. 526.

OCRIS HEAD Aughris, Each-ros, the promontory of the horse,

County Sligo. Battle of Each-ros in 598. Site of a monastery. An unusual chasm at the base of the cliff, which causes a great noise heard along the coastline for many miles, known as the Coradh Dtonn (pronounced Cora Dun). Natives can forecast the weather by the volume of sound of the Coradh Dtonn. Pl. 55.

OWBAWN WEIR County Galway, Fair Owen's Weir, locally known as Dun Eoin; on the edge of Dubh Loch or Dhulough which Lady Gregory in *Seventy Years* says was the Dun of King Guaire the Hospitable, who ordered the drowning of the mother of St. Colman in the deepest part of the river in Coole. M. 65.

OX MOUNTAINS Sliabh Ghamh, County Sligo, the stormy mountain. The name was incorrectly thought to be Sliabh Damh – meaning Ox; approximately parallel to the Atlantic Ocean from Collooney to Ballina. The Hawk's Well, Hawk's Rock, Hart Lake, and Heart Lake all in the Ox Mountain range. M. 201, 203, 207, 209.

PAIRC-NA-CARRAIG Literally the Rock Field, but known to employees as the Fox Rock. One of the Seven Woods of Coole, County Galway. The river flows under high poplars on a steep bank by Pairc-na-Carraig. C.P. 469.

PAIRC-NA-LEE Pairc na Laoigh, the calves field. One of the Seven Woods of Coole, County Galway. C.P. 469.

PAIRC-na-TARAV The bull field or park. A field surrounded by an unusually high stone wall used for exercising a bull is very often called the Bull Park. One of the Seven Woods of Coole, County Galway. C.P. 469.

PATRICK STREET Dublin. In the Liberties outside the old walled city. The Cathedral of St. Patrick, the largest church in Ireland, and of which Jonathan Swift was Dean of the Chapter 1713–45. His monument with that of 'Stella' is in the South aisle. Yeats often sat there meditating. Marsh's Library, the oldest public library in Ireland (1707) nearby. A. 203. M. 52.

PILOT HOUSE Rosses Point, County Sligo. There were two Pilot Houses but the one referred to by Yeats is the small ruin of four walls with two small circular windows looking out to sea near Elsinore; both on the left hand-side of the road as one goes from the village to the beach. A. 267.

THE POST OFFICE O'Connell Street, Dublin. The classical columns of the facade of the General Post Office (1814–18) by Francis Johnston, stand out in majestic dignity. As a result of being the headquarters of the insurgents in 1916, and having the Declaration of Independence read there, and being bombarded again in 1922, all that remains of Johnston's work is the O'Connell Street front. In the main hall, stands the 1916 bronze memorial statue, *The Death of Cuchulain*, by Oliver Sheppard whom Yeats knew at the Metropolitan School of Art. C.P. 373, 375. Pl. 435, 704. B. 12.

PUCK FAIR Killorglin, County Kerry. The annual Aonach an Phuic is held in mid-August. The highlight of the fair is the crowning of a white male goat, as king, to preside in the square over the three day's fair. Origin of custom doubtful; thought to be pagan. Pl. 684.

QUEENSTOWN County Cork. Named after Queen Victoria (1847). Previous to that, and since 1922, named Cobh (pronounced Cove). Important naval base and place of embarkation. M. 34. E. & I. 343. A. 526.

RACHLIN Rathlin Island off the coast of County Antrim. Called Rikina by Ptolemy. Reachlainn, or Rechru in the *Annals of Ulster*. One of the islands to which the Fir Bolg retired after the battle of Moytirra. Brecain, grandson of Nial of the Nine Hostages, drowned in the channel. St. Columcille founded a monastery there. Rathlin was the first place in Ireland to be ravaged by the Vikings. Robert Bruce stayed in a castle on the island where he is alleged to have observed the proverbial spider. In Elizabethan times the whole population was massacred by English forces. C.P. 442.

RAHASINE Rahasane Park was originally the name of a French family's estate about two miles from Craughwell, County Galway. Pronounced 'Ration'. M. 29.

RAPHOE Rath Bhoth, the ring fort of the huts, County Donegal. Monastery founded by St. Columcille or St. Adomnan who also wrote St. Columcille's life. A. 506.

RATHBROUGHAN, Rathbraughan, Berchan's Rath. Beside the borough boundary stone on the old Sligo–Bundoran road. Fort Louis, a long one-storey building on the banks of the Rathbraughan river, is where Matthew Yeats (1819–85) great uncle of the poet lived. A. 20, 53.

RATHGAR A suburb of S. Dublin adjoining Rathmines. In 1883 the Yeats family moved to No 10, Ashfield Terrace, Rathgar. A. 79.

RENVYLE Rinn-Mhil, Mil's point, Connemara, N. County Galway : home of Yeats' friend Oliver St J. Gogarty. Yeats and his wife George "got in touch with a ghost which haunted a room in the old house". Augustus John's last portrait of Yeats (1930) painted here. Ex. 310.

ROCK OF CASHEL, See CASHEL. Ex. 266.

ROSCOMMON Ros Comain, St. Coman's Wood. The county town of that name. Ruins of a 13th c. castle, the original of which was built by the English as a Connacht outpost to curb the O'Conors. Ruins of the Dominican Friary on the site of a 6th c. monastery founded by St. Coman; interesting altar-tomb of the 13th c. founder, Felim O'Conor, King of Connacht, with figures of gallowglasses on the base.

Douglas Hyde (1862–1949), the friend of Yeats, was born at the Rectory at Frenchpark; later lived at Ratra. After being first President of Ireland (1939–45) he retired to Ratra, where he is buried. A. 227, 253.

ROSSES POINT Ros Ceide, County Sligo, small seaside village, five miles from Sligo, where the Yeats family spent their summer holidays with their Pollexfen and Middleton cousins. Now very changed from the rustic village which the poet wrote about and Jack painted. A. 7, 15, 18, 19, 31, 46, 51, 52, 61, 68, 73, 76, 78, 129, 206, 258, 262. M. 88, 89, 90, 92, 93, 94. C.P. 20. Pl. 641. B. 26. V. 9. Ex. 407. E. & I. 513.

ROTUNDA Alongside the Rotunda Hospital (1751) in Parnell Street, Dublin. Now the Ambassador cinema; originally built by John Ensor (1764) as a Supper Room for the Assembly Rooms and ballroom, in part of which is now the Gate Theatre, founded in 1928. The tradition of the Irish theatre revival has been carried on there in the work of Hilton Edwards and Michael MacLiammoir. Ex. 98, 134.

ROUGHLEY Raughley, Raghling, Reachla, a promontory in County Sligo N. of Drumcliff and Lissadell. The home of the O'Beolains, Erenaghs of Drumcliff. The ruins of Ardtarmon Castle, residence of the Gores before Lissadell was built and also of the earlier Dunfore Castle of the O'Harts, owners of that district before their lands were confiscated.

It is at Roughley pier that the Pilot boards ships to guide them to Sligo Quay. A. 73. M. 95, 96, 191.

ROYAL DUBLIN SOCIETY at Balls Bridge, Dublin. Founded 1731. Apart from its other activities of an antiquarian nature and to which Yeats refers, it is best known for its Annual International Horse Show. A. 203.

ROYAL IRISH ACADEMY 19, Dawson Street, Dublin. Founded by royal charter 1785. Ireland's leading learned society. Over 1,200 MSS. Best known are *The Book of Ballymote* (14th–15th c.), *Book of the Dun Cow* (11th–12th c. literary codex), *Book of Lecan* (14th–15th c. literary codex), *The Stowe Missal* (8th–9th c.), a *Psalter*, possibly written by St. Columcille, (6th–7th c.) and *Annals of the Four Masters* (1632–36). E. & I. 511. A. 186, 516.

ROXBOROUGH Craig-a-Roiste, Roche's Rock, County Galway. Granted (1686) to Dudley Persse, Dean of Kilmacduagh, whose father, John Persse, according to tradition, came to Ireland with Cromwell. Name changed to Roxborough (1707) – an interesting union of part of the Irish name with 'borough' added. Between Loughrea and Gort, where Augusta Gregory (née Persse) was brought up. Had been a flourishing 6000 acre working estate, pleasant demesne with trout stream, good grazing, old trees, walled garden, bounded by Slieve Echgthe moorlands. The house commandeered by IRA (1922), then looted by a gang of thieves who burnt it to the ground. Only a gable and a chimney stand. A. 385, 392, 394, 456. C.P. 150.

RUTLAND SQUARE Dublin, mid-18th c. square named after the Duke of Rutland, Viceroy of Ireland. Now Parnell Square; N. end of O'Connell Street. See MUNICIPAL GALLERY OF MODERN ART which is on N. side. A. 367.

ST. COLMAN'S WELL County Galway. Numerous wells dedicated to the Saint in the diocese of Kilmacduagh, but the one indicated by the text is in the townland of Corker in Kiltartan where the Saint was born and was placed under an ash tree by his mother. She was in hiding at the time and wanted to baptise the child, but there was no water nearby. However, a fountain miraculously gushed forth under the shelter of the tree. The ash tree had disappeared by the time *The Cat and the Moon* was written (1925) but Yeats obviously knew of the legend. Pl. 461.

ST. JOHN'S CHURCH John Street, Sligo, now the Protestant cathedral; originally designed by Richard Cassel but remodelled in Perpendicular Gothick (1812). Built on the site of a Hospital founded (1223) by Clarus Mac Maillin, the founder of Trinity Island Abbey, Lough Key.
    The poet's parents were married in St. John's. George Pollexfen's funeral with Masonic rites is described by the poet (A. 67–74) and William Pollexfen, his grandfather, supervised the building of his own mausoleum in the churchyard. A. 64, 68.

ST. STEPHEN'S GREEN Dublin. Once a common, the first and largest of Dublin's squares. Includes many 18th and 19th century houses on the perimeter. In the gardens, laid out in 1880, are several monuments, including Edward Delany's Wolfe Tone monument and one by Henry Moore in memory of W. B. Yeats. Ex. 222.

ST. TERESA'S HALL 36 Clarendon Street, Dublin, where *Cathleen ni Houlihan* had its first public performance with Maud Gonne playing the title part (1902). After these performances the Irish Literary Theatre became the Irish National Theatre. Ex. 89, 100.

SALLEY GARDENS Some say that those referred to by Yeats were on the bank of the Garavogue river opposite the Imperial Hotel, Sligo. It is more likely they were on the bank of the Ballysadare river between the Ballina road and the mills. There was once a row of small thatched houses on this bank of the river, and each of these had a salley (willow) garden to provide scollops for the thatch. A tradition in the village holds that Yeats when young was accustomed to meditate on a big rock in the river, in view of these gardens. The poem (C.P. 22) is little altered from the folk original. C.P. 22.

SANDYMOUNT CASTLE Sandymount Green, S. Dublin. This castle was owned in 1865 by Robert Corbet, the poet's great-uncle when the poet was born at a small house in Sandymount Avenue nearby. The castle was an 18th c. house gothicized with Abbotsford-type battlements, tower and cloister. The gardens were large and it was landscaped with vistas down to the sea, with lake and small deer-park. After Corbet's death it was sold and in 1900 the poet visited it again, but could scarcely recognise it as it had been split up and built over. Ex. 318, 319. A. 394. C.P. 370.

SCALP An ice age gorge, the name of a townland in Slieve Echgthe, County Galway. M. 253.

SEAVIEW In the townland of Cregg, between Rosses Point and Drumcliff, County Sligo, where great-Aunt 'Micky' Yeats lived (Described A. 19) A. 51.

SCANAVIN County Sligo. The Well of Scanavin, tober sceanm-han, the well of the fine shingle. Tubberscanavin is a small village on the Sligo–Dublin road about one mile from Collooney, County Sligo. C.P. 50.

SHAN-WALLA County Galway. There are two explanations for this name : the first that it is called after an old wall (Sean balla), the other, according to Mr Mulkere, the son of one of Lady Gregory's Irish teachers, that the original avenue to Coole House ran through it, before the Gregories made two new avenues. He identified it as the old road, sean bealach. One of the Seven Woods of Coole Park, County Galway. M. 62. C.P. 469.

SLEUTH WOOD See SLISH WOOD M. 175. C.P. 20.

SLIEVE ECHTGE, See ECHTGE.

SLIEVE FUADH Sliab Fuait, the highest point of the Fews in County Armagh, where Conall Cornach guarded the borders of Ulster in *The Tain*. Alleged to take its name from Fuait, son of Breogan, who was killed there : the scene of *The Chase of Sliab Fuait* in which Ailna changed himself into a deer to trap Finn and the Fianna. Also associated with Naisi and Deirdre in *The Fate of the Sons of Usna*. Fingin, the weird physician of Sliab Fuait, healed Cuchulain of his wounds, and Cuchulain caught his war horse, Liath Macha, at Loch Liath on Sliab Fuait, to which he returned after the death of Cuchulain. Sid Finnachaid the abode of Lir, father of the children of Lir was near the mountain. Pl. 669, 699. VP. 802.

SLIEVE G-CULLAIN, old name for SLIEVE FUADH. VP. 802.

SLIEVE LEAGUE Sliabh Liag, the mountain of the flagstones. In S.W. Donegal on Atlantic coast. The cliffs, 1,972 feet high, the tallest marine cliffs in Europe. Remains of a monastic settle-ment with oratories and Holy Well on the summit, associated with St. Assicus. M. 86.

SLIEVENAMON Slieve-na-Mon and Slieve-na-Man, County Tipperary. Sliabh na mban or Sliabh na mban Feimhenn, the mountain of the two women. Te and Men wives of two bards of the Tuatha de Danann. Mentioned in *The Pursuit of Giolla Dacker and his Horse*. C.P. 115. M. 337. Ex. 29. E. & I. 236, 512.

SLIEVE OCHTE, See ECHTGE. Ex. 40.

SLIEVOUGHTER RANGE Yeats says this range is near Roxborough House, County Galway. But the only range of hills near Roxborough, is Echtghe, now Slieve Aughty, called Slieve Baughty in some older writings. No local inhabitants know of any part of Echgthe ever being called Slievoughter. It may be a corruption of 'Slieve Aughty' as it may have sounded to Yeats when spoken. A. 392. Ex. 40. See ECHTGE.

SLIGO Sligeach, the shelly river, referring to the river Garavogue which drains Lough Gill into Sligo Bay. Sligo was always an important site because of its strategic position on the ford of the route from Connacht to Donegal. Its emergence as a town came about in 12th c. when Maurice Fitzgerald built the first fortified castle. Thereafter it became a prize between the contending forces of the O'Donnells of Donegal and the O'Conors, Sligo. The control of the town from the castle continuously changed with the fortunes of war.

The best description of modern Sligo is perhaps that of Sean O'Faolain in *An Irish Journey* (1940).

"Myths suffuse the air like spray. They fall on the simplest things and cover them like hoar-frost or the shimmering webs that mist the fields in Summer. The eye obscures itself. Objectivity is impossible where so many reliques excite the mind; dolmens, cairns, stone circles, forts, cromlechs, trilithons, all suggestive of events not merely great but superhuman. One look at that flat-topped plateau of Knocknarea, one hint of its associations, one glimpse of the enormous cairn surmounting it – as large at close quarters as one of those man-dwarfing slag-heaps of the Black Country – is enough to subdue all disbelief; and

81

since it is one of the first natural objects to catch the eye one approaches this region subject to it even before one has well entered it.

It is a lovely site for a town, the Garavogue broadening into a bay; big steamers lining the quays, the old seamens' pubs, small, very cosy at night, with squared windows facing the river where the lights from the opposite side fall daggering into the water. Here and there the streets widen into something that is almost a square, and in so small a town to meet unexpectedly the Abbey, the Cathedral, the lovely Norman Church of St. John's, several lesser Churches and Chapels, gave added force to the first impression I got of a varied and articulate society with a tradition behind it. It is a welcoming town. In others, through the west I have felt "This is remote, but I feel no sense of loss". Here I did not once even think that I was remote. There was, more than in any other place that I have been of its size, an extraordinary feeling of self-sufficiency. And when I began to consider this, and wonder why it was so, I could only think that this is because the life modes are more varied here than in those other places because there is a variety of classes, and traditions – the best Protestant stock in all Ireland is in Sligo – and because of that surrounding dignity of history and fable which tempts one to liken this little port to some port-city on the Piraeus where the gods smiled on every hearth, or thundered in every storm, and no man thought that there existed beyond the hills any world but his own."

The oldest name of the Garavogue River, Fluvium Sligeach or Sligeach, changed to River Gitly – Gitly being a corruption of Gilly, the name given to the river because it flows from Lough Gill.

SLISH WOOD Stretches along the lower side of the Killery Moutains at the edge of Lough Gill, from near Dooney Rock to Inisfree, County Sligo. The name derived from the Irish word "slios", meaning "sloped" or "inclined". Yeats refers to this wood as Slish, the usual name for it, but in 'The Stolen Child' (C.P. 20) he calls it 'Sleuth Wood'. This in turn is derived from an Irish word "Sliu" meaning a slope or slant Although the name Sleuth Wood seems unknown to residents in that locality, it is possible the poet heard it so called by local inhabitants. A. 72.

SPIDDAL – An Spidéal, The hospital. A Gaelic speaking coastal village in County Galway. One of the best known Irish language study centres. Ex. 252.

SUGAR LOAF Beannach Mhor, the great peak, County Wicklow. The mountains are known as The Great Sugar Loaf and The Little Sugar Loaf. Ex. 321.

TARA Temair, Teamhair, a place with a view, County Meath, 6 miles S. of Navan on the Dublin–Navan Road. The inauguration of the King at Tara, called Feis Temro, symbolised the mating of the new King with the local earth-goddess, and was destined to bring fertility to man and beast in his reign. This particular pagan fertility rite, Medb, is last recorded as late as 500 in *The Annals of Clonmacnois*.

Founded by Slainge, the first Firbolg King; Ollaimh Fodhla convened the first great Feis at Tara. Tuathal Teachmar, High King A.D. 85, convened the States of Ireland in assembly at Tara. Cormac Mac Art responsible for many regular assemblies for promulgating laws for all Ireland. Kings of Ireland called Kings of Tara long after it ceased to be the residence of the king.

According to the Annalists, the heyday of Tara was in the times of Conaire More, Cormac Mac Art, Nial of the Nine Hostages and his son Laoghaire, who confronted St. Patrick at Tara. The Annalists record the cursing of Tara in the 6th c. by St. Ruadan for violation of the right of sanctuary by the High King. Modern historians prefer the theory that Tara declined as a pagan centre with the coming of Christianity, although it retained its mystical significance into mediaeval times.

Tara today is a network of earthen mounds, depressions, ramparts and ditches, some of which have been excavated, and proved to be Iron Age. Originally a cemetery like other Irish cemeteries where Aoenaghs were held, it developed into a royal site. Tara figures in many of the ancient sagas, and although now a mere grass-covered hill, conjures up a picture of the legendary splendour of romantic Ireland.

The Lia Fail brought to Ireland by the Milesians on which kings of Ireland were inaugurated was on the mound now known as The Mound of Hostages. It was possibly taken to Scotland for use there in the Irish Kingdom from whence it was then taken to Westminster Abbey where it lies today under Edward the Confessor's Coronation Chair. But the whole story is doubtful.

Tara's Halls were not built of stone and so are no more. Only the great earthen mounds indicate their sites.

A poem preserved in *The Yellow Book of Lecan* (14th c.) contains detailed plans of the banqueting hall of Cormac Mac-Art, 3rd c., giving the seating arrangements and the portions of meat due to each class, e.g. Ollave poets got a steak, but minor poets got only crooked bones, as did the historians. C.P. 374, 503, 504, 507, 509. Pl. 645, 648, 656, 657, 658, 659, 663, 666, 676. Ex. 14, 15, 83, 200.

TEAMHAIR, See TARA. Ex. 14, 15.

THOMOND Prior to being formed into County Clare in the 16th c. it was a much bigger territory. Until the reign of James I it was part of Connacht; then it was added to Munster. The Dal Cais was the paramount sept. The Mac Clancy's kept a school of law at Knockfinn; referred to in *Annals* as ollaves or hereditary Brehons of Thomond. The lands of Killilagh were held by them free of rent by virtue of their office until end of the 16th c. The school was renowned throughout Ireland. They lost all in the Cromwellian settlement.

The Margraths were ollaves of Poetry in Thomond, Tuath-Mumhain, North Munster.

The Contention of the Bards collected into a volume of 7,000 lines in the 17th c. was written by Teige Mac Daire, ollamh of Donough O'Brien, 4th Earl of Thomond, and answered by Lughaidh (Lewy) O'Clery, Ollamh of the O'Donnells of Donegal. Soon all hereditary poets of Ireland joined in The Contention. It was the last flickering of the hereditary Bards, conducted in the official metre and style of bygone days, before it was extinguished in the Cromwellian Wars. Teighe possessed the castle and estate of Dunogan by right of his office as ollamh of Thomond. Pl. 439.

THOOR BALLYLEE, See BALLYLEE.

THORNHILL Sligo on the Strandhill Road, the first of a pair of Victorian three-storeyed semi-detached houses on the left-hand side of the road after passing under the railway bridge. In Yeats's time was the home of George Pollexfen, the poet's uncle and then about a quarter of a mile into the country. A. 69, 255, 257, 262, 407, 409.

COUNTY TIPPERARY Tiobraid Arann, well of river Ara, name of a small town and fertile County in Munster, prominent in the history of Ireland. Grave of Gobaun Saer at Derrynavlan. Gaelic Athletic Association founded (1884) in Hayes Hotel, Thurles. Birthplace of the Fenian, John O'Leary (Yeats' friend) (1830–1907) and Charles Kickham, novelist and Young Irelander (1826–1882). A. 211. E. & I. 259.

TIRARAGH Tireragh, barony in County Sligo between Ox Mountains and the sea, called after Fiachra Ealgach, son of Dathi, King of Ireland, Tir-Fhiachrach-Fiachra's district. The MacFirbisi, also descended from Dathi, were hereditary historians to the O'Dowds (Kings of North Connacht) and kept a school of History at Lecan in the barony of Tireragh, where they compiled *The Great Book of Lecan*, and *The Yellow Book of Lecan*. The latter contains the earliest extant form of *Táin Bó Cuailgne*. Duald McFirbis, the last of his family, compiled *The Book of Genealogies* and *Chronicon Scotorum* during the Cromwellian Wars. C.P. 25.

TIR CONAILL, Tir Chonaill, see DONEGAL. E. & I. 362.

TIR NA nOG – Thír na nóg The Land of the Young where Oisín was enticed by a fairy lover and lived until the coming of St. Patrick A.D. 432. Ex. 8, 9, 392.

TRINITY COLLEGE Dublin. Founded 1592 by Queen Elizabeth I, for the education of Protestants, on the site of a 12th c. Augustinian monastery. None of the old buildings remain, but the fine 18th c. buildings with splendid classical facades and elaborate interior plasterwork, flanked by extensive playing-fields, occupy a large area in the centre of Dublin. The library houses Ireland's greatest collection of books and MSS including *The Book of Kells* (illuminated 8th c. gospel book); *The Book of Armagh* (9th c. gospel book, with the only surviving early Irish copy of the New Testament); the so-called *Book of Leinster* (11th c. literary codex). Alumni of Trinity College mentioned in Yeats's writings include Jonathan Swift, Oliver Goldsmith, Edmund Burke, George Berkeley, Wolfe Tone, Henry Grattan, Robert Emmet, J. M. Synge and Oscar Wilde. Three previous generations of the poet's family had graduated there, but he did not follow them as he realised he was unfitted for some of the academic work. When Yeats was writing the introduction to *A Book of Irish Verse* (1895) he thought Trinity College an 'enemy of all enthusiasm' and was strongly critical of its attitude to the Celtic revival. Later he modified his views when he came to admire its 18th c. graduates – Swift, Goldsmith, Berkeley and Burke. In 1922 he was given a D.Litt. degree by the College. A. 79, 91, 233, 343, 394, 399, 456. M. 9. E. & I. 298, 338, 397, 399. Ex. 281, 322, 323, 409.

TORY ISLAND Toraigh, a place of towers, 9½ miles N.W. of Horn Head off the north coast of County Donegal. Three miles long, 785 acres, associations with the legendary Balor the one-eyed giant. Balor's Castle, Prison and Fort. Columcille founded a monastery here in 6th c. The first part of Ireland that Yeats saw when he woke up after a night in the Liverpool–Sligo boat. A. 50.

TUAM County Galway, Tuam da Gualann, the tumulus of the burials mounds. Monastery founded by St. Jarlath, 5th/6th c. became important ecclesiastical and educational centre. Attained its peak when Turlough O'Conor, King of Connacht (1106–56) and High King of Ireland, centralized the kingdom of Connacht at Tuam, erected a cathedral and commissioned the Cross of Cong, one of the glories of Irish medieval art, for it. A. 412. M. 9.

TUBBER The Well, a village in County Clare. Pl. 92, 103.

TUBBER-VANACH Not possible to place precisely. It means Holy Well or Monks Well and might be any of the numerous wells in Ireland. Pl. 3, 304.

TULIRA CASTLE Tullira, near Ardrahan, County Galway 16th c. Burke Castle, 'remodelled', to the horror of Yeats, 1882. The home of Edward Martyn, one of the founders with Yeats and Lady Gregory of the Abbey Theatre; himself a playwright, author and patron of the arts, particularly of music and stained glass. Today it alone remains of the three Galway great houses, Roxborough and Coole Park being no more. A. 372, 376, 385, 398, 425, 426, 427.

TULLAGH – Tulla, an Tulach, a village in County Clare where Biddy Early lived. M. 184.

TWO ROCK MOUNTAIN Three Rock. A mountain near County Dublin one part of which is known as Two Rock Mountain and the other part Three Rock Mountain. E. & I. 413. C.P. 135.

TYRONE – Tir Eoghain – the territory of Eoghan, a son of Nial of the Nine Hostages, progenitor of the Ui Neill or O'Neills, Kings of Ulster and sometimes High Kings of Ireland. Now reduced to the County Tyrone. A. 70.

ULADH ULSTER Coicid Ulaid named after the race of people which ruled. When Yeats refers to Uladh, it is to that province before it was divided in 5th c. by the Ui Neill, and still ruled from Emain Macha; that is to say it is the Ulaid of the Ulaid Saga Cycle, consisting of Northern Ireland. But at the time the Sagas were written the Ualdh of which they wrote was no more; it was then confined to a small district equivalent to the modern County Down, with Downpatrick as its capital. The Heroic Age of the Sagas ended with the Destruction of Emain Macha, 450 A.D.; the Sagas mostly the product of the monasteries were written during the Christian era in Ireland. The heroic centres of Ireland such as Emain Macha, Tara, Cruachain and Ailenn had ceased to be centres of importance except in a symbolic sense.

The modern word "Ulster" is a combination of the original Ulaid with the Scandinavian addition of "Ster" meaning province.

The Annals of Ulster are the oldest and most reliable and were used as the basis for the majority of the other Irish Annals. Pl. 171. M. 118. C.P. 91, 459, 461.

ULSTER BANK AT SLIGO A small building on the corner of Stephen Street, and Markievicz Road, facing Douglas Hyde Bridge across the Garavogue River.

The Bank's semi-circular windows made Yeats think of it when he saw the Royal Palace at Stockholm, though with regard to the size of the two buildings the comparison is ridiculous. A. 542.

UPPER ELY PLACE is a short continuation of Ely Place, Dublin. George Moore once lived at No 4 and Yeats's friend Oliver St J. Gogarty on the opposite side of the road. The garden at the end of the cul-de-sac once George Moore's, later Gogarty's, is now with what was Gogarty's house the site of The Royal Hibernian Academy of Arts. A. 443, 444.

USNA Uisnech, a place of fawns, County Westmeath, originally in the province of Connacht. The Hill of Uisnech was regarded as the centre of Ireland where the Tuatha de Danann paid annual tribute to the Formorians. The site of one of the great fairs or cenaghs which indicate that it was originally a cemetery. Its pagan origin is confirmed by the fact that it was one of the sacred places with special fires connected with Druidical rites and the source of all secular fires. The incident of the Pascal fire lit by St. Patrick at Slane, in defiance of the fire at Tara, emphasises this.

The centre of Ireland was marked by The Rock of Divisions

(Aill na Mureann), now known as the Cat Stone, set in one of the numerous earthen mounds on the Hill of Uisnech. This was the meeting point of the five provinces called by Giraldus Cambrensis, The Navel of Ireland.

King Tuathal the Acceptable built a palace here in 1st c., and instituted the annual Oenagh (fair) held on May Day.

In 15th c. a Lord Lieutenant plundered the O'Higgini, the hereditary family of poets at Uisnech. In retaliation the poet satirised him, as a result of which it is said the plunderer died five weeks later.

The Fate of the Sons of Uisnech the finest of the Ulster stories preserved in *The Yellow Book of Lecan*. The oldest copy of this saga, in the Royal Irish Academy, was copied by David O'Duigean at Shancough, County Sligo, in the late 17th c. He was the last of the O'Duigenans of Kilronan and Castlefore, Hereditary family of Chroniclers associated with several old Gaelic compilations, notably *The Book of Ballymote, The Annals of Loch Cé* and *The Annals of the Four Masters.* C.P. 41. M. 227. Pl. 173, 199, 202, 704.

USNACH, See USNA.

VALLEY OF THE BLACK PIG is an undefined valley in which a battle will be fought. There are the remains of the Black Pigs Dyke in Co. Cavan, Co. Longford and Co. Leitrim. VP. 808. C.P. 73, 526–7.

WATERFORD Port Lairge. The Capital of County Waterford, a town of Viking origin. Strongbow landed in Waterford, butchered its citizens and married Eva, daughter of Dermot McMorrow King of Leinster to strengthen his claim as successor to the Kingdom of Leinster. It gained the title Urbs Intacta from Henry VII in return for its fidelity during the Lambert Simnel campaign in Ireland. Beseiged by Cromwell. Thomas Francis Meagher, Young Ireland leader born here, as well as many international scholars particularly of the 16th and 17th centuries. The Waterford Glass industry founded in the 16th c. Reginald's Tower (1003) converted into a civic museum in 1955. Ex. 75.

WELL OF BRIDE Tobe Bríde, Tubberbride or Tubber-
breeda, Collooney, County Sligo. The townland takes its name
from a Holy Well dedicated to St. Bridget. The well was in a
fort with a souterain (an underground stone built passage), which
was closed up and later broke out in the bowl of a big old
sycamore tree near the spot. It remained there summer and
winter for over 100 years until the tree fell in a storm (1974).
M. 243.

WESTMORELAND STREET formerly called Sraid an Fheis-
tighe, Dublin. Named after a Lord Lieutenant of Ireland. Links
O'Connell Street with College Green, developed, circa 1800,
by the Wide Street Commissioners as a street of shops with
uniform frontages. A. 370.

WEXFORD Loch Garman, Garma's inlet. The name of Danish
origin. A County on the east coast of Ireland. The first landing
of the Anglo-Normans in 1169 was at Bannow Strand where
they built their first castle and town in Ireland.
    The mother of William Pollexfen was of County Wexford
origin. A. 9.

WICKLOW Cill Mantain. St. Mantan's church. The word 'Wicklow' is of Danish origin. According to tradition both St. Patrick
and his predecessor Palladius landed on the Wicklow coast, but
were driven away by the local chief. The stronghold of the
O'Byrne clan who continually harassed the English Pale from
its mountain fastnesses, and where Red Hugh O'Donnell found
refuge after his escape from the dungeons of Dublin Castle. The
massacre of Glanmalure (1601) ended the threat of the Wicklow
Chieftains. M .47. V. 167.

WINDY GAP Bearna na Gaoithe. Innumerable places of this
name throughout Ireland, but the one referred to by the poet
is that where the old Sligo road meets the railway bridge in the
townland of Carrickhenry opposite Carraroe Church, Sligo.
Elsewhere referred to by the poet as the Gap of the Wind.
M. 243, C.P. 129. V. 167.

YELLOW FORD Beal-an-atha, Bhuidhe, the mouth of the yellow ford, on the river Callan, County Armagh; where the Great Hugh O'Neill defeated the English army (1598) under Sir Henry Bagnall, whose sister Babel had previously eloped with O'Neill. Bagnall was on his way to relieve the siege of Benburb by O'Neill. A well known poem is "The Lament for Owen Roe O'Neill" by Thomas Davis, the Young Ireland poet. A. 35.

YORK STREET Dublin, a street leading from Stephen's Green at The College of Surgeons corner. John B. Yeats had a studio, John O'Leary presided over a Young Ireland Society, and James Clarence Mangan worked in a solicitor's office in this street. A. 65, 90, 99.

YOUGHAL Eochaill, The Yew Wood, County Cork.
Set by a fine harbour this walled town was incorporated by Royal Charter in 1462 when it was owned by the Earl of Ormond. Sir Walter Raleigh was granted a large tract of land here after the Desmond Rebellion. Cromwell landed here (1649) and made it his winter headquarters. Ex. 124.

BIBLIOGRAPHY

Alphabetical Index to the Townlands and Towns of Ireland (1901)

Byrne, F.J., *Irish Kings and High Kings*, Batsford, London (1973)

Craig, Maurice, *Dublin 1660–1860*, Hodges Figgis, Dublin, (1969)

Curtin, Jeremiah, *Myths & Folklore of Ireland*, Boston & London (1890 and 1911)

Dillon, M. and N. Chadwick, *The Celtic Realms*, Weidenfeld & Nicholson, London (1967)

Dineen's *Irish–English Dictionary*, Educational Co. of Ireland, Dublin (1927)

Fahey, J. A., *The History of Kilmacduagh*, Gill & Co. Dublin (1893)

Frost, James, *The History of County Clare*, M.R.I.A. Ascot Press (1893)

Gregory, Lady I. A. *Seventy Years 1852–1972*, Colin Smythe, Gerrards Cross (1974) and Macmillan, New York (1976)

Gwynn, Stephen, *The Fair Hills of Ireland*, Maunsel & Co., Dublin (1914)

Hardiman, James, *The History of the Town and County of Galway*, Folds & Sons, London (1820)

Jennett, Sean, *Connacht*, Faber, London (1970).

Joyce, P. W., *The Origin and History of Irish Place Names*, Longmans, Greene & Co. London (1902)

Kilgallon, Thady, *The History of Sligo*, Kilgallon, Sligo (1926)

Killalin, Lord and M. V. Duignan, *The Shell Guide to Ireland*, Ebury Press, London (1962)

Kirby, Sheelah, *The Yeats Country*, Dolmen Press, Dublin (1962)

MacCana, Prionsias, *Celtic Mythology*, Hamlyn, London (1970)

Mac Liag, *Cogadh Gaedhil re Gallaibh (The War of the Gaedhil with the Gaill)*, Longmans, London (1867)

MacLiammoir, Micheál, and Eavan Boland, *W. B. Yeats and his World*, Thames & Hudson, London (1971)

Nic Shiubhlaigh, Maire, *The Splendid Years*, Duffy, Dublin (1955).

O'Donovan's Letters for Counties Sligo and Galway, Ordnance Survey (1835, 1927)

O'Grady, Standish, *History of Ireland*, Ponsonby & Co., Dublin (1881)

O'Rorke, Dr., *The History of County Sligo*, Duffy, Dublin (1889)

Pollock, J. H., *William Butler Yeats*, Talbot Press, Dublin (1935)

Praeger, Robert Lloyd, *The Way That I Went*, Hodges Figgis, Dublin (1937)

Rogers, Mary, *Prospect of Erne*, B. N. I. Printing Co., Belfast (1967)

Walsh, Fr. Paul, *Irish Men of Learning*, Sign of the Three Candles, Dublin (1947)

APPENDIX 1

Notes on G. B. Saul's *Prolegomena*

George Brandon Saul's two *Prolegomena*, to Yeats's Poems and Plays, have a number of errors and omissions; those I have noticed I give below. The page numbers are those of the University of Pennsylvania Press editions – 1957 and 1958. For the place names, see the relevant entries in the text, when no explanation is given below.

POEMS

page

46   Inver Amergin is Arklow, not Inber Scene, as Saul says.

49   Salley Gardens. Salley means 'willow' here. Every thatched house had its own salley garden to provide scollops to hold the thatch.

50   Fr. Hart lived at Cloonamahon, two miles from Collooney until he was dispossessed, when he went to live at Killaser on the Armaghmore estate of the Otharas. Cloonamahon has been a monastery since about 1940.

50   Boreen : is a narrow road or lane, trees are not necessary.

54   Inisfree is mentioned in the *Four Masters* under 1244 A.D. If the island were other than Inisfree, Yeats would not have to walk so far and the place known as Yeats' Bed where he rested, could not be where it is.

60   Ballad of Fr. Gilligan. The original story is in O'Rorke, I think.

64, 79, It is not correct to refer to fairy folk as side (the plural
178, 188 of síd, a fairy mound or dwelling place). The dwellers

94

in side were sidhe. (Saul has it right on pp. 90 and 184.)

90   Not Aoife, but Aoibheal, a mythological person; though Murrough, son of Brian Boru is historical.

Craig Liath. Is not Carrick-lee, but the Grey rock, the sid or residence of Aoibheal.

90–91   Goban = Goibniu. There is an old ruin on the side of Slievenamon alleged to be one of many built by the Goban Saor, scattered from Antrim in the north to Kerry in the south.

95   Leebeen. Is a very small fish, the first fish very small boys hook, put in jam jars, take home and let die.

95   Guaire is an authentic King of Connacht, called Guaire the Hospitable, who lived at Gort where he entertained the poet and his retinue. See also Lady Gregory's first play *Colman and Guaire*.

96   Cruachan is not the same place as Croghan (a village near Elphin in Co. Roscommon). However it is known today as Rathcroghan; the site of the ancient capital of Connacht and the one always referred to by Yeats.

115   Cashel was the seat of the Kings of Munster for centuries, until it was given to the Church in the 12th Century by Cormac Mac Carthy King of Munster, who was responsible for building Cormac's Chapel, not restoring it.

117, 119, 135   The Countess or Madame Markievicz, was never known as Con Gore-Booth Markievicz.

123   Salmon falls. The famous salmon falls in Co. Sligo are at Ballysadare. The Sligo ones are insignificant, and they can be discounted, as falls.

174   "cleft that's christened Alt". Is not known for any magical associations.

176   Ben bulben is Beann Ghulbain or Binn Ghulbain and is

traditionally associated with the wild boar hunt in which Diarmuid was killed.

182 Bera of ships. Not modern Dunboy, but near it.

186 lee-Lighe. Not grave, but calves' field.
carraig. Not a headland or cliff. Here rock or large prominent stone.
Inchy, inis. Not 'perhaps' but *is* a special word for water meadow.

PLAYS

page
27 Tubber-vanach and Carrick-orus. See the relevant entries in this book.

28 Allen is the legendary Almhuin, but the Bog of Allen is the central boggy plain of Ireland.

29 Flowery Plain. May be a typographical error for *Towery*. Moytura is derived from either Magh Tuiridh, a plain of pillars, or Magh Turach, a towery plain.

32 Ballygawley Hill. Is five miles from Sligo on Slieve Daene, not the town in Co. Tyrone.

35 Enniscrone.

35 "white-scarfed riders". It is the usual practice for young men in rural Ireland to wear white bands or scarves on one shoulder across the breast and tied under the other arm with a black ribbon, at funerals, usually those of young men, and tragic deaths. Compare "A Political Meeting" in *Life in the West of Ireland* (Dublin 1912) by Jack B. Yeats, to illustrate the manner in which the scarves were worn at funerals. Yeats could not be referring to priests here.

| 37 | Tubber. Actually in Co. Clare. |
| | kippeens. Really small sticks fircones etc., used for kindling a fire. Used for fircones at Coole. Not ham bones. |

37   Tubber. Actually in Co. Clare.
kippeens. Really small sticks fircones etc., used for kindling a fire. Used for fircones at Coole. Not ham bones.

40   Gort is considered to be a town.

61   Kilcluan.

66   Aughanish

72   Bawneen. A flannel bawneen cannot possibly be a small enclosure. Correctly it is the sleeveless coat worn by the men of Aran.
Muckanish, Bailevehan, Aughmana.

73   Thomond.

96   The grey of Macha. Kelpie is a scottish word. Curiously, although there are sightings of this animal in the West of Ireland (see Monsters and Sheoguey Beasts section in Lady Gregory's *Visions and Beliefs in the West of Ireland*), it has no name as such.

APPENDIX 2

Ancient Names for Ireland

From earliest times historians and poets have written of Ireland
under many names. Homer and Plutarch called it Ogygia. Caesar,
Tacitus and Pliny called it Hibernia, while Aristotle and Shelley
called it Iernia. Other names given it by poets include, Inis na
Veeva, Insula, Sacra, Juverna, Iverna Hiera, Erin, Eire, Banba,
Fodhla, Scotia, Inisfail and Roisin Dubh (Dark Rosaleen) Yeats
of course used Cathleen ni Houlihan.

APPENDIX 3

A note on Pronunciation

F. J. Byrne says in "Irish Kings and High-Kings" : – "Irish phonetics are not simple, and Old and Middle Irish are bedevilled by a peculiar orthography based on the British pronunciation of Latin in the fifth century". Modern Irish has the additional complexity of three dialects, Ulster, Connacht and Munster with their differences in pronunciation.

Irish place names go back to the time of the first colony to come to Ireland. At least four place names derive from colonists. Other place names derive from members of the four later colonies. Thus most of the current Irish place names belong to the period of Old or Middle Irish and in many cases have a local pronunciation incapable of generalised guide lines.

The danger of attempting a useful Glossary for Irish place names is obvious. For this reason we have decided against one.